What O

About Earth and Sky

"Guy went through the worst-case scenario for anyone who strives to believe in the goodness of God. And yet it was in this dark place that he found God at His best. This book will not only captivate you with Guy's story, but forever change how you view God."

BEN ARMENT
Creator of STORY and Dream Year
www.dreamyear.net
Author of *Dream Year: Making the Leap from a Job You Hate to a Life You Love*

"Along with his thoughtful intentionality, Guy Delcambre is a storyteller. He can make you feel like you're sitting in his living room, yet simultaneously leave you breathless—it's a rare talent that few possess. Guy's book, *Earth and Sky*, is a stunning work full of some of life's hardest and most joyful moments, all written in his unique, masterfully poetic voice. This book is a true gift and a must-read for any who have walked the paths of grief, doubt, and faith."

NISH WEISETH
Author of *Speak: How Your Story Can Change the World*
Editor in chief of deeperstory.com

"With vulnerability and raw honesty, Guy lets us in on his journey of grieving the loss of his wife and the 'perfect' life they shared together, of discovering his need for a greater understanding of God, and the relationship between the two. Whether you're in the midst of loss or simply feeling far from God, I highly recommend this book to anyone needing a reminder of His sustaining presence."

JUSTIN LATHROP
Strategic Solutions
justinlathrop.com

"Guy Delcambre is a widowed, single father of three young daughters, and a minister who has been given the extraordinary talent to express his life experiences and grief journey in honest, striking, and encouraging word pictures. His story touches the hearts and souls of both mourners and their caregivers. It guides readers through a story of loss that includes not only deep sadness but joy, peace, and hope for the future. His words from the depth of his grief and faith are compelling, enlightening, and inspiring.

"It has been my privilege and honor to accompany Guy and his three lovely daughters for over two years on their grief journey. It has also been my privilege and honor to witness Guy and his family begin to heal and to live lives that are examples for other mourners. I highly recommend this book for those struggling in grief after the death of a loved one and for those who care for those suffering after the death of a loved one."

LARRY M. BARBER, LPC-S
Certified Thanatologist
Director, GriefWorks, Dallas, Texas

GriefWorks is a grief support ministry for children ages five through eighteen and their adult family members who have experienced the death of a loved one.

"In *Earth and Sky,* Guy Delcambre delivers a soft and winding sort of genius, the kind that brushes aside time and space to isolate the substances that move people—love, companionship, loss, grief, death, and most importantly, resurrection. This is more than Guy's personal story of living beyond loss, it's a decree of hope that all of us can be well."

SARAH CUNNINGHAM
Author of *Well Balanced World Changer*, and blogger who seeks to stir extraordinary friendship in a sometimes too ordinary world
sarahcunningham.com

Earth and Sky

A BEAUTIFUL COLLISION OF GRACE AND GRIEF

GUY DELCAMBRE

Contents

To Elizabeth Marie, Emily Anne, and Chloe Grace,

three little, sweet souls who followed closely

through the darkest of night—all is not lost.

All is never lost.

These words are yours, to remember

always how we made it out,

and never to forget Grace's rapturous embrace.

First, the Epilogue

> Beneath clouds and moon and stars
>
> on an empty shore we met crashing waves,
>
> our promise broken,
>
> my words wavered,
>
> I just need to be found.

MY EYES OPENED SLOWLY, unknowingly to a new world. "Hey, you need to come with me. *Now!*" John's voice had a measured urgency that wasn't normal for my friend. "The nurse sent me to get you. It's time. I think this is it. It doesn't look like she's going to make it. I don't think she'll be with us much longer."

The weight of this was impossible.

It's the hardest thing to find something when you can't see.

Like when you first wake up from a deep sleep or when you stumble through a dark room looking for something in the place you last left it, in what has been its regular place in your life. It is traumatizing and disorienting when what you are searching for is not in the place you expect it to be.

Faith. Trust. Hope.

Fading.

Time slowed.

Each breath was measured and deep.

I had known this time would arrive, but it seemed to find me too early. I felt lost and disoriented.

Five days earlier, my wife, Marianne, had been rushed to the hospital. She was admitted to the ICU floor, and since then her life had delicately swayed back and forth. During those days, I had quickly lost my way . . . and myself. Suddenly, my mostly undisturbed and enjoyable path—the one that had always seemed to sprawl out much farther than I could ever see—was enveloped in a dense fog that ended at the edge of a cliff. I had never been in this position before. I was used to seeing what was coming and adjusting accordingly. But here, there was nowhere to go. I could think of no prayer that would reveal an inviting detour around the dead end.

I tried to be brave, but my heart melted.

I tried denial, but my heart was reminded that this was real.

I tried faith, but my heart shrank, dwarfed by fear.

All I could do was watch and hope to be saved.

The day before Marianne died, I walked outside and sat on a bench. I couldn't stand to be in the hospital anymore. The rhythmic sound of the ventilator that was pushing air into my wife's body, the beeping sounds of IV machines filling her with medicine, and the rotation of loved ones to accompany us on this terrible journey was just too much. I couldn't take another hug or look into another pair of pity-filled eyes. The silence in my heart was driving me mad. I walked out of the hospital hoping to hear something different. Alone in the warm sun, I could feel each of my heartbeats, one by one. But I couldn't express what I felt in my heart with each beat. In one moment, I imagined Marianne as she struggled to open her eyes. As her eyes adjusted to the light, our eyes made contact and a warm smile crossed her face, suggesting all would be well, all would be as it should be. But in the next moment, all I could feel was the vast emptiness of life without her. I was back at the cliff in the fog . . . completely lost.

Maybe God would heal her and use her story as an amazing example of His unending faithfulness and activity in our ordinary lives. Surely He would intervene and rescue her—despite lab reports, scans, and medical professional opinions. After all, that's the way it should be. Those are the stories we hear of faith overcoming what appears to be hopeless circumstances. Those who believe in God escape tragedy. But still I thought, *What if I'm the exception?*

What if God doesn't transcend tragedy for me?

What if she doesn't make it?

What does that mean for our family, our daughters?

For the future we dreamed of together?

For all the work and ways we were faithful?

Yes, certainly because of our diligence and faithfulness, she will pull through. In the five days leading up to this moment, I did what anyone would do: I begged, I pleaded, I bargained, I yelled, I cursed, I cried, I sat alone in silence, and I felt like each word and emotion disappeared into the sky where the air is thinner and the dead escape to rest.

And then, sitting in the warmth of the sun on the bench just outside the hospital, a thought softer than all the rest somehow interrupted. It was as if God precisely placed this thought so deep in my heart that I couldn't deny the certainty of it—like the air I was breathing.

The thought was simple and short. Actually, it was less of a thought and more of a sense of knowing. I suddenly and internally understood that I wasn't going to leave that hospital with my wife. And I knew that I would never have the chance to walk this earth with her again. That echoing, impossible-to-ignore thought took my heart to a depth both lonely and cold.

I knew all of it. I knew too much all at once.

I knew I could do nothing to change our circumstances.

I knew I was not going to win this time. No matter how hard I tried or what I said.

Still, I frantically searched my thoughts for the right Scripture, for the right prayer, for the right promise. But there was nothing. Every time, I came up empty. Memories of our life together flashed through my mind like lightning splintering across a disturbed sky.

I couldn't stop thinking of Marianne's smile. Her words echoed in my wilting heart like symphonic tones, beautiful and warm. "I love you, stud," she would say with a smile that beat upon my heart like relentless waves on the shore.

I felt abandoned.

I felt betrayed.

And I felt too overwhelmed to know exactly what I felt.

I vividly remember walking to her room that morning. I understood the time had come. John had told me she was fading. This news was just as definite and sure as the quiet thought that God dragged across my heart two days before. I knew this was it. I had arrived at the line that I feared most, where earth and sky meet, where life as we know it here resigns to death.

My wife was dying.

I could do nothing about it but breathe and wait and try to find just enough space to be okay. In mere moments, our lifetime together would come down to one final breath, and we would be separated by the only thing that could overcome us: death.

I remember the day we got married. We waited for what seemed like a lifetime for that day. We had talked and dreamed and hoped about what the day would be like.

Marianne had worked diligently to put all of the pieces together for our wedding. It was going to be just as we wanted it. When the day finally arrived, all the pieces were pushed into place. Our friends and loved ones soaked up the warmth with us, all of us basking in the glow of love and potential. I had never felt so much love in all of my life.

Everyone seemed to be genuinely happy for us. Several friends hugged me and affirmed that Marianne and I made so much sense together.

I grinned like a giddy schoolboy as her dad walked her down the aisle. Marianne glided past our friends and family with a grace I imagined only angels could have. Her eyes glowed with life and love, and her smile was as inviting as the rising sun on a cool morning.

I stood still in my tuxedo, watching her get closer. My heart was on fire. We smiled nervously throughout the whole ceremony, wishing in unison for the shared lifetime before us to begin.

That day felt like a dream—a dream you want to live in—where the sun is warm, the pace is slow, and everything falls on the right side of the line. We held hands. Each passing moment felt full and forever.

But now I was the one walking toward her, down the hall of the hospital. And there was no grace in my movement as I approached her room. I kept thinking, *wishing* I were dreaming. I *must* be dreaming. Surely, this isn't real. This can't be the end of our story.

I can't breathe.

The air is stale and old, familiar with the life I once knew so well and loved so completely, but can no longer find. This life fades into the night, disappearing and leaving only me in place.

I want to see her alive, unharmed and unclaimed by death, waiting for me as she always did, with a smile. She was so good at being only herself. And herself is what found me.

Now I'm shuffling along with legs too weak to carry me another inch, closer to the end. I know life, in some semblance, will continue after this particular closure, but this sense of ending is so decisive I can't envision what might lie beyond. It's cold, colder than a northern wind stealing your breath and cutting deep to your bones.

This end is my beginning, though I don't yet know it. I can't yet understand any time or progress or middle to this suffering. And I certainly don't comprehend what kind of life might be in front of me.

I'm grasping for what is fading, like a child trying to hold smoke or catch fireflies. But what I reach for evades me. This ending is happening, thrust upon me, whether I comprehend it or not. No word or act of agreement deviates death's course, though I've tried. Death is intent on winning, on completion. In this moment, what feels sure is that God has miscalculated or misjudged . . . or misled me. The preciseness of where He is doesn't matter much. He's not where I need Him to be. Or so I think. And so I accuse.

Everything is so sterile and clean. I can barely stand it. The antiseptic, washed-out environment tries to cover up all that feels dirty and wrong with death.

I know everyone dies. Don't we all? It is just that she shouldn't be dying or dead or gone. Not yet.

"Where will I find anything without her?"

She is I, and I am she. We are one. How do you take away half of one and still remain whole?

Why was I led here? Why do I have to let go?

Who is God, really, to watch in stillness and silence?

How do You love me, us, and them?

I think about our children . . . they will never understand. This is their nightmare: to lose their symbol of stability forever without saying goodbye, to part ways without a mother's kiss.

God, the cost they will pay is too much for me, Your accepted son, to bear. That loneliness and tragedy and sadness will rip straight through their souls. I wish I could swallow that bitter reality pill that will separate earth and sky as far as night and day for them. If possible I would fall on that grenade to keep their hearts from exploding. If I could trade places with her, for them, I would. I would never want to leave her and them alone. But You know that, don't You? And maybe that's why. If so, that's a horrible reason.

Yet here I am. I remain now, soon to be fully alone, torn with a clouded but grateful heart, I think. In a way, small yet distinct, I'm glad to be the one left behind. I would never want her to have to sink deeply into the dark alone. I would never want her to have to hold them and support them on her own.

Maybe I'll wake at some point, a cold sweaty mess, fully relieved that this was the worst dream my darkest subconscious could ever create. I would dream that dream every night for an eternity if I could wake to find my world still undisturbed and in place . . . to see her smile . . . just one more time.

But I know I'm not asleep. I just woke up. I can smell the sterile, clean environment of the hospital trying to convince me all is well while tragedy rips away the thing that defines every area of my life.

Surely the rudder will turn and she will narrowly skim the edge of the earth and return back to us. There's no way that God would allow this to happen to me when all I've tried to do is give my life to Him.

I've tried to quietly and faithfully serve Him. But maybe it doesn't matter. Maybe life and death burn uncontrollably— contained, but not controlled.

After what felt like an eternity, I arrived at Marianne's room in ICU where she had been for nearly five days. Sympathetic looks from the hospital staff both crushed me and enraged me. Lonely violence gripped my heart instead of the calm, peaceful acceptance you hope to experience in those moments.

I walked into her room and asked everyone to leave. And for the first time in over a decade, I stood alone. The aloneness settled on me with the weight of a thousand days.

Not every story resolves the way you wish it would. Not every ending is happy. Sometimes the credits roll unexpectedly, leaving plotlines unfinished and precluding further questions. And then, the end.

II

"Where were you when I laid the earth's foundation?
Tell me, if you understand. . . .
Who laid its cornerstone—
while the morning stars sang together
and all angels shouted for joy?"
JOB 38:4, 7

What is life about and what is its value?

When you are sewn to someone who dies, you can't escape the moment. All you know about life and purpose is called back to the drafting table.

We build kingdoms in careers, houses, dreams, and possessions. We find love and determine what we desire. Those things define us, and we call it life. When those things leave us, we call it death. What we know and learn, what we can see and control, we call earth. What we cannot, we call sky, or heaven, or forever . . . or nothing.

Fullness of the truest, most unmistakable kind exists in the moments when life meets death, earth meets sky.

When we become aware of death, life takes on more value. We're forced to acknowledge something bigger at work, active beyond the existence we take to be everything. Suddenly, everything we reached for and attained, everything that satisfied us—and everything we reached for and missed—is reduced to things and moments.

Love remains. Love and the knowledge that maybe that's all that was real in the first place. Maybe earth is just a frontier being resettled and redeemed in our hearts.

What I called "life" had been calm and peaceful. My days passed, warming safely in the sun, familiar and friendly. I was blessed with ease and love and comfort. I had a wife who truly and fully loved me, and together we learned how to love and live.

Everything felt graceful, sometimes unnaturally so. We experienced seemingly little resistance to the good we lived. And we always overcame the minimal resistance we faced. We were in love with each other, with God, and with all that He meant to us.

We never had a home nestled in a quiet suburb, perfectly landscaped, manicured with bright flowers and shady trees, positioned within a perfectly kept, white picket fence. But we felt like we lived in a picture . . . a perfect picture. And looking back at the bumps and bruises we experienced in our life together, the strength we gained from going through each trial made life seem even more perfect.

Many times, friends and acquaintances commented on how perfect our life seemed and how good we had it. We exchanged deep smiles and agreed wholeheartedly.

I had most of the things that I needed, and I was reaching for what I wanted. I was confident that in the end, no matter the circumstance or difficulty, everything would work out and be okay. If the waters became rougher and the waves more threatening, most problems were only temporary, and the storm would eventually yield to sunshine.

I regularly recognized God's apparent hand in my life. I had good reason for optimism. I thanked Him for protecting me, my family, and the life that we were building. Things were going so well that my life seemed to be on autopilot. Rarely was there reason for alarm or concern.

I was indeed thankful for God's presence and direction in my decisions, but day to day I was mostly on my own . . . unless I really needed Him, of course. Then He would gracefully enter, and things would be okay again.

In the world I knew, God was a saving God, rescuing those in need. He had famously sent His Son to save the world. But I never fully understood His ability to save until I became hopelessly lost, until I pleaded for rescue from fear and loss and accusations in the new, unfamiliar day. On that day, I was desperate.

What do you do when life doesn't add up?

What do you say when the heavens are hauntingly silent?

Where do you go to escape the life that is eerily fading to mere memories, leaving you with only pictures and pieces?

How do you reconcile a deep-seated trust that has been invaded by tragedy?

God is the sovereign, majestic, mysterious King. He doesn't exist because we created Him; we exist only because of His grace.

He has always loved us. He always will. But He's not our waiter or butler or maid.

Words like *good, love,* and *happy* are very real, but we tend to define them based on our experiences. It's not that they don't have autonomous and independent meaning; they do. But we understand them far better in the context of their opposites. Those words have meaning, too—words such as *bad, hate,* and *sorrowful.*

In the darkest night, alone and lost, I found God . . . or perhaps I should say He found me. One way or the other, I was found, and that was all that mattered.

God has a magnificent way of redeeming what is broken and wrong. His love and goodness flood into our lives, constantly challenging, changing, and reshaping us. I'm learning to live in His redemptive broad strokes as well as in the fine details of His artistry in my life. Pain and loss have become my greatest treasures. Through the experience of overwhelming tragedy, I have experienced God to be something different, something greater, so much more than I ever imagined.

> In the depth of the darkest night,
> tighten your hands to the smallest light . . .
> small enough to invade your heart,
> whole enough to heal what is a crumbling mess,
> able enough to hold the world ignoring.

I had always been slightly mistaken about exactly who and what God is. Even the tiny detail of referring to God as "He" pushes my understanding off just a bit. The description of "He" is understandable because it's part of the human context. But God isn't part of the human context. He created the human context. He described Himself this way to help us comprehend Him.

The way we understand God is based on how He has chosen to reveal Himself to us, but God is so much more than what we can understand about Him. I understood God to be personal and relatable, a friend—the God who chooses companionship with those He creates. But God isn't limited to being my personal God. Or, I should say, that's not *all* He is. God isn't the God of my life alone. He's so much more. He's the God of the universe where my life exists and is sustained.

If He were merely the God of my life, He would be subject to my judgment. If He were only my friend, He would exist for my comfort and entertainment. If He were limited, then I would be on my own in this universe, left to fate and chance—a more overwhelming cosmic swelling tide than I ever imagined. However, if He is indeed the God of the universe, if every person and circumstance is subject to His existence as the source and creator and author of life, then I am a piece of the fabric of His cosmic creation.

I am sustained as part of all that He is sustaining.

I am well taken care of no matter the terrors that threaten.

After all, what tragedy can possibly threaten a cosmic ruler? What horror can disrupt His ability to tend to His world? Through the experience of tragedy, God has not become depersonalized in my life. Instead, He has become more complete in my thinking and relation to Him. I have become more personal to Him. He makes Himself small for my sake, but He is not small, not at all. For a long time, I had it wrong. Previously, I knew God as small—

small enough to be held in the space of my heart. But now I know He is infinitely larger and ultimately complete.

His ability to take care of us needn't be questioned. God exists outside and beyond all that unfolds in our lives. In Him we find our beginning, and through Him we discover there is no end—not even in death.

III

This book is not about death. This book is not about grief. This book is not about sadness and all the prickly little things associated with it.

It is a remembering and an acceptance of moments when boundaries were pushed back, when darkness succumbed to light and life swallowed death. It is a confession of God, present and very near, sustaining life by all means necessary, a revealing of Himself through abundant grace.

It is ultimately about life, love, grace, and being found. That wasn't clear to me when I first started composing words and recollecting memories. It's clear to me now, although the clarity doesn't make the remembering much easier.

Be my shelter,

and may Your heart be my home.

Give me rest from the swelling storms;

quiet my violent mind,

which hates easily and lusts for control.

Sweep the dust that has gathered on broken floors,
carry it out back and burn the pictures;
spread the ashes over fertile soil.

May the dimming light in my eyes
be swallowed by the warmth of a new dawn.
Let the pieces of broken bones be collected;
plant my heart deep within Your ground
so that it may never again be found.

My hands are untrustworthy
and my steps are unsteady.
My eyes lie often and my lips know no good.

But only keep me here,
in the eternity of Your shadow,
where grace breathes strength invincible,
where stained hands are held, not broken.

CHAPTER TWO

Adorned in Her Jewelry

MY DEAR SWEET BABY GIRL, ELIZABETH . . .

This past week you had your first recital, and it was so cute!!!!!!!!!!!!! I could not smile big enough. I was so proud of you, you did so well, and you were so excited and proud of yourself. Watching you on stage made my heart melt! You are now 4 and will be 5 next month, and it tears me up that you will be in kindergarten soon. How did this happen so fast!? I am watching you develop, and I see what a sweet and beautiful girl you are, inside and out. You tend to be shy in some situations, and at the same time very silly, and very outgoing!

You are so good to your sisters—a little mommy for sure. There are times when you share so well with Emily that it surprises me. Like when you get candy at school, you hand it over when she cries because she didn't get one. It is clear you love your sisters very much. You love to be the helper and are always ready to help me. Now, you aren't the perfect little angel. I have seen you many times tease Emily . . . just because. You always make me smile, and we are always so proud of you. This whole year of pre-school you have never gotten in trouble! You are very respectful, and I am so thankful for that!

You love our youth group, especially Jenna. You also love some of the boys. In fact, you shared with me last night that you were going to marry big Josh. Anytime the youth come over, you are on cloud nine! To you it is the very best thing that can happen. You get a lot of attention from them, and they really love you. I, too, love you more than words could ever express. Both your daddy and I pray always for you and your sisters. We pray that you would walk in God's perfect will and that you would serve Him with all your heart. I pray that you would know that God loves you, and so do your mommy and daddy. You are such a blessing to us. I thank God for you.

I love you so, so much, Elizabeth Marie!

Mommy

. . . . .

My dear sweet Emily,

You are always full of so much energy, and you always keep people laughing. You are just so cute that I can hardly stand it sometimes. There are so many funny things that you do that I really don't think I could list them all. At this time in your life, you are full of energy and always dancing, and now all of a sudden you are in this whining time. Everything seems to be drama, drama, drama! Every time you pray at dinner or at bedtime, you pray for your dog to come back and to get better . . . even though we don't have a dog.

You will start at Leblanc's Learning Center in the fall, and you are so excited. Although I wonder how much learning you will do. You tend to be pretty stubborn, and at times you refuse to listen when I am trying to teach you something. For example . . . when we go over our abc's, you correct me, as if I don't know them, and then you come up with a, g, h, c, and even an 8 gets thrown in. You also seem to have developed your own counting system. Even though I go over it again and again, you will not acknowledge the #2. It usually goes something like this . . . 1, 4, 3, 8. It is so funny because I will even have you repeat it with me—even with something as simple as 1, 2, 3, you throw out 1, 4, 8. You are very smart, though. You have an amazing imagination, and there are certain things that you pick up right away. You have just chosen to make up your own alphabet.

You are such a great little sister who loves to be taken care of by her big sissie. I love sitting with you and using our imaginations. And you are such a wonderful and creative artist!! Well, my sweet girl, your mommy and daddy adore you. You are so precious to us. I love you so much, Emily Anne! We have the most incredible baby girls. I pray that you will always serve the Lord with all your heart and that you will fulfill all that God has designed for you. I also pray that you always know how much we love you. It has been the most amazing blessing to me to have you girls. I am truly so blessed and so very thankful.

I love you so very much, honey!

Mommy

. . . . .

My dear sweet Chloe,

I can't believe that you are already 3 months old! Time is already flying by. On May 3rd you turned over all by yourself . . . what a big girl :) You had really been trying, and it seemed that at any moment you would do it. Sure enough, there it was! Now, at this time there are a few things that are certain . . . you love to look at lights, you smile and coo at them. It is very cute, but the rest of us are jealous . . . you seem to like them more than any of us. You are so cute and just such a beautiful baby girl. We adore you! You are smiling and cooing all the time (especially at the lights). You are so precious to us. I can't imagine what we did so long without you. I love you so, so much, Chloe Grace!! I pray that you will serve God with all your heart, and that you will always know just how much God loves you, and how much your daddy and I love you. . . .

I don't even know where to begin. Time is flying by and you are growing up so quickly! At times my heart just breaks to realize how fast this is all going by. I pray I will remember it all and that I will savor each moment. You are talking so much now—coming out with the craziest things . . . followed by the craziest expressions. All of you girls are so dramatic! Just this past Sunday you were talking with your pac-cah and ma-nah about your hair and discussing how your morning went as you were getting ready for church . . . you finally ended with saying your hair was "freakin' weird!"

You have this great lisp . . . you sometimes sound German, and other times you sound like Sylvester the Cat. You stick out your tongue when you say your "s" sound, and it is the cutest thing!

Now Chloe, there are so many more things to share about you . . . I will say you happen to be quite bossy . . . not at all intimidated. You and your cousin Audrey can be the best of friends and at other times the worst. The two of you can really fight it out. We are desperately working on your manners. You tend to fall apart when you don't get your way. There are other times, however, when you are so tender and loving. You love to cuddle! You are very affectionate! You like to give kisses . . . big ones! You always make your sisters laugh when you grab their faces and give them

a big smooch! You LOVE to make others laugh . . . if
someone is laughing, that is your cue to keep going! :)
    Now, another thing you love is food. One Sunday
while you were in your class, your teacher was
discussing joy and what it means to have joy. When
you were asked what gives you joy, your first answer
was "food." I'm not surprised! :)
    I love you my sweet Chloe!
    Mommy

                    • • • • •

My three girls are their mother's daughters. Marianne's love for
them was direct and influential. The spark that illuminated her
heart so brightly flickers and grows within them. Their mannerisms,
thoughts, and smiles all reflect her. It's beautiful to me.

I know they wonder and quietly fear forgetting her. Sometimes
I hear it in their questions. They were forced to let go without one
last goodbye, and it haunts them. I do my best to hold them and
look into their eyes, the ones that so clearly reflect her, and assure
them they can no more forget her than forget themselves. Within
such a short time, she imprinted the fullness of her heart on theirs.
Each step they take is inspired and shaped by her love for them.

She is gone now, no longer present in each of their days. She
didn't leave us or relocate. She died, suddenly and unexpectedly.
Nothing can prepare you for a day like that. And nothing seems to
hold you together in the days that follow. Imagine being a kid who
feels like she has everything she needs, only to come home at the
end of an ordinary day to a totally different life.

A picture of my three daughters hangs in my house. It was taken a few weeks after Marianne died. My daughters are standing still, radiant and beautiful against an aged and battered wall. They are holding onto each other like they mean it, like they need to. Their faces glow with a contentment that seems almost misplaced, even inappropriate for that occasion in their young lives. The emotion of that moment is forever captured. I often sit and stare at their faces.

The picture was taken when good family friends, Mel and Kim, came into town for a weekend visit. Before they came, Kim asked if we would be interested in having a family photo taken. A friend of hers is an amazing photographer and had offered to do a full shoot for us at no cost. Immediately, I agreed. To capture the images of my girls during this point in their lives meant the world to me.

I decided to let them pick out their own clothes for the photo. I told them, "Wear whatever you want. Pick out your favorite outfit—something that you feel beautiful in." Then I brought out Marianne's small jewelry chest and told them to pick out any of her jewelry that they wanted to wear. They were so excited for their "photo shoot," as they referred to it. They felt special. They needed to. I needed them to.

It amazes me how alive they were in that moment, especially because of all that had just been stripped from them. I was sure I was not as resilient.

It was just the four of us now, and things still felt awkward and out of place. My greatest fear was that they felt as disturbed and disrupted as I did nearly every minute of every day. Anxiety over their healing and grief kept me up at night and woke me early in the morning. I prayed and begged God to somehow hide their eyes from the reality of the loss and to comfort their hearts, but my prayer felt like a foreign language to me.

Ever since Marianne had passed, most of my thoughts had focused on these three little souls and the path in front of them. How do you tell three little girls who dream of princesses and happy endings, whose hearts are innocent and free of the terrors of night, that their mother is gone? And how do you look into their perplexed but loving eyes and explain that by "gone" you mean dead? My wife, their mother, had died just two months before they posed for the photo shoot. It seemed like only two hours earlier.

· · · · ·

It was a Monday when Marianne took her last breath. It was quiet in her room. She slowly, peacefully exited this world with a grace common to her.

Then she was pronounced dead. That was it.

I asked the nurse to turn the machines off—the ones that had kept her alive for nearly five days. She did, and then left the room, leaving me alone with my wife's body.

It was the quietest moment I had ever had with her.

She was motionless because she was gone. I was motionless because I felt paralyzed by the weight of facing a life I didn't recognize and was overwhelmingly unprepared for.

Even then I knew the first step would be the most difficult. I knew I had to go and tell our little daughters what had happened, and I didn't have the words for the conversation.

I don't remember walking out of the hospital. The first thing I recall is waving goodbye to Marianne's aunt and uncle as I drove away. I drove home only half aware of normal life going on around me. I was leaving the hospital, exiting that painful place, but entering something new. I was reentering the world as a widower, but more importantly, as a single dad to three innocent little girls. The world and life that awaited me was no longer one I knew or understood.

I drove home in silence, hearing only the hum of the tires on the road. I was heading toward what I fully expected to be the most difficult, and possibly the most damaging, conversation I would ever have with my daughters.

I searched for the words to say . . . anything . . . but nothing came to me. I was blank. It was as if my thoughts dared not even go there . . . as if they protested even verbalizing this new, unchosen, uncharted world.

The next thing I remember was getting out of my car and walking down the sidewalk to my sister's house. My girls had been staying there while Marianne was in the hospital. It had been nearly a week since I had seen them and since they had seen Marianne. They had no idea how much their world had changed.

The girls were busy with the activities of a normal day . . . coloring, cartoons, snacks, toys. All was frighteningly normal. For all they knew, Mommy would walk through the door, smile glowingly, and sweep them up in a warm and familiar embrace.

That would have been normal. But things weren't normal any more.

Instead of the two of us greeting them, it was me—only me—who walked through the door. I tried to be confident, reaching to be strong, while failing at both.

"Dad, you're here!" they yelled with excitement.

Leaping hugs ensued as they engulfed me with all the energy that had accumulated during the week we were apart. For a moment, I was raptured back to the world I knew when they would run to greet me as I came home from work.

But that world—and the loving memories of it—vanished with the words that followed. "Where's Mommy?" our oldest daughter, Elizabeth, immediately asked.

"When is Mommy coming home from the hospital?" Chloe, our youngest, echoed. Their voices were thick with excitement.

I couldn't even swallow. The moment was so much more terrible than I could have imagined.

Emily, our middle daughter, was quiet. I had a hard time meeting her eyes. I could tell she knew something was wrong, very wrong, as she backed into the shadows of her heart. She tried to avoid being part of what was happening.

My heart crumbled and quaked inside my chest. They had no idea how dark the day was and how different their lives had become.

Their questions about their mom landed like stabs to my chest, violating the sacredness of our family, our togetherness. I was sure I could see life dim a little in their eyes as they saw the loneliness in mine.

"Let's go outside. I need to talk to you, girls."

"No!" screamed Elizabeth. "No! Where is Mommy? Is she dead? Did she die?!!"

I was paralyzed. Words failed to come, or maybe I just didn't want them to come.

Either way, I didn't say anything.

But my eyes had betrayed me. They said what my mouth could not say . . . would not say. The quietest pain escaped Elizabeth's mouth: "Don't you tell me she died. Please don't tell me that."

The other girls just stood there frozen. Tears began to stream down their faces. Slowly, quietly, their hearts were being violated. Death was present and bigger than any of us.

I didn't say anything. I still couldn't.

My little girl was asking a question, demanding answers that were complex, textured, and laced with death.

We walked out onto the patio with my mom and sister. The three of us held them tight as hope, life, and light let go. I grabbed them close to me and held them one at a time. I told them the saddest thing their ears would ever hear. I felt helpless, alone, and—most of all—unbelievably angry with a God who would sit idly by and let this happen.

Expletives thundered in my heart in response to a pain too big for me to comprehend.

The strangest part of my conversation was that I was trying to tell them something I wasn't sure I believed myself.

"Is this really happening? This can't be real!" It wasn't just the death and loss that were hard to fully own; the hope that the girls and I would recover seemed just as elusive.

I had always felt like I wasn't honest with them every time I assured them Santa Claus was real or the Tooth Fairy had left the dollar under their pillow. But I never thought it would feel like a lie when I tried to insist God would provide a rescuing grace, that He would somehow reconstruct our broken and bleeding lives.

I spit out the facts. I told them Mommy had gotten really sick and the doctors couldn't save her even though they tried their best. I told them she was in heaven now, and she wasn't coming back.

I said all the things you're supposed to say in the moment—the moment that's never supposed to happen.

I had never felt farther from faith than in that moment as I watched death force its influence upon my three innocent girls.

In that horrible moment, I knew our definition of life was readjusting in their minds and hearts. I knew that things would never be the same for us again. We sat there for what felt like forever.

I held them tightly, over and over. Each time they became quieter and quieter. And my heart grew lonelier and angrier and more confused.

The only thing I felt I could control was how they thought. So somehow, in a moment of divine grace, words appeared . . . words meant for them . . . the insulating words I was so desperately looking for. Surely this was the result of the thousands of people praying for us.

"God didn't take Mommy from you. He doesn't need her in heaven. He would so much rather she be here with you. And I think His heart is sad because He loves you so, so much. Mommy was sick, so sick that the doctors couldn't do anything to help her. They tried everything. God didn't take Mommy from you. He wouldn't do that. God rescued Mommy from the pain of her sickness. Instead of allowing her to keep hurting and feeling pain, God took her to heaven so she wouldn't hurt or be sick anymore. I love you so, so much."

I told them we would see Mommy again—maybe not for a long, long time, but we would meet her again. I told them God loved them and we could always trust Him to be good. No matter what the day looked like, God would always be good.

. . . . .

Another photo hangs just below the one of my three daughters. It's a picture of the four of us. The girls, dressed in outfits they chose are radiantly adorned with the miscellaneous pieces of Marianne's jewelry as we sit together in an empty field.

The picture shouts that life has become different.

Marianne was such a force of gravity, such a vibrant, life-giving strength in our family. She was a remarkable mother and a wonderful wife, the most beautiful person I knew. She moved through life with effortless grace and delicateness in each step and word. Knowing her changed you. You wanted to smile with her, and you felt better when she smiled at you. And it is with a similar, familiar delicacy that the girls rest on my arms and shoulders in the picture of the four of us in the empty field, slowly filling with life again.

As they surround me in the picture, their smiles are even more beautiful than the jewelry they wear. It's hard to capture the emotions that swell in my heart as I look at that picture on the mantle in our living room. It's one of the first records of our life together after Marianne's death. They had lost a mother. I had lost a lover and a friend. Yet there they were, adorned in her jewelry, smiling defiantly with a grace that transcended the massive changes in our lives.

I smile with deep emotion every time I gaze at that picture, thankful for that moment forever captured. It was one of the most special days of my life for reasons that ripened and echoed in the days ahead of us.

Slowly, the pieces of life came back together. Everything didn't always fit exactly and line up perfectly, but like a patchwork quilt, our family began to cohere again. Some parts of our routine, of course, were similar to what they had always been, but at other times life felt foreign and different, like an alternate universe mimicking what we had previously known.

Little things mattered much more than they used to. Items that hadn't mattered much to me, like the objects Marianne used to touch, meant everything to me now.

I was the only parent the girls had now, and I quickly discovered my limitations. When we were two parents, we operated as a team. I was lucky to have such a good teammate. Marianne was irreplaceably amazing as their mom. Now that it was only me, I felt completely lost as a parent. I didn't know how to do it alone. The girls and I weren't used to interacting without her.

They were used to having us both, not only me.

I overcompensated and tried to fill the void by being super dad. To deal with the pain of loss, the sting of death, and my new insecurity in parenting, I kept myself busy, insulated from a withering heart.

I could feel my wounds late at night when the kids were in bed and the house was quiet. It was an uncomfortable silence that consumed my security and reduced me to a desperate plea that wouldn't be quenched. I wanted what I could never have again.

Marianne no longer existed in this world. I was alone. And I hated being alone.

I buried the pain as deep as I could and tried to ignore the path behind me with two sets of footprints, our footprints together. I did all I could to lose myself in busyness. I didn't fall apart, melt down, have a dramatic mental break, or exhibit erratic behavior. I didn't have the luxury of those options. I had a great responsibility to three little lives. I knew they would take their cues from the way I lived. To escape my pain, I lived small and far away from the vulnerable parts of myself. I prayed prayers that would keep me a healthy distance from the horrible darkness in my heart and dreams. And I prayed that God would protect my daughters' hearts, walk with them through each day, and help them not to be scarred by the wound. I pleaded for their lives to stabilize, for the strength to endure, and for the wisdom to find a way forward.

I was playing a role. I was living for my daughters, trying to be everything I thought they needed. Meanwhile, the surface layer of protection I had constructed around my heart was growing thinner and the darkness was pushing up with violent effort. I was growing more numb each day.

And it was killing me.

Living for my daughters, for their happiness, for their future, for their security, seemed more than honorable and heroic—it was everything. It was all there was to live for, all that mattered. They were all I had left that was identifiable and real.

I remember my best friend, Shawn, telling me a day or so after Marianne's funeral that I should expect to feel raw emotions, and that I should allow them. He was right, of course. I felt like I was sinking under the loss and the pressure of holding our family together. Emotions erupted from me in response to the inconsolable grief. I didn't know what made sense anymore. I could no longer deal with life at a distance. My heart was growing too thin, and it was bleeding out, bursting in odd, unplanned moments. Something deep down was not being comforted and healed. Exposing it was too threatening. I was suffocating under the weight of grief, heartache, loneliness, hurt, and anger. The weight was like a silhouette—a shadow following me—present constantly but without handles. I was ignoring, neglecting, and distancing myself from it. It hurt too much.

God has a way of finding you, and He will, even in your worst moments. I began to realize that no matter how hard I tried, my daughters still felt sorrow that I couldn't seem to reach in our conversations. Gradually, they stopped talking to me about their hurt, and they hid their tears.

My heroism was deeply flawed. Unknowingly, my behavior added to their insecurities. I was trying to live for them, but I was avoiding the hurt I felt. I wanted to be their counselor, their hero, and their rescuer, but instead I became someone they instinctively didn't feel safe around. They knew I was dying inside, so they tried to protect me by hiding their fears and tears.

My behavior may be understandable, but it didn't help my children or me. Avoidance is a quick fix, but it causes long-term damage. Grieving is the only way to deal with loss and death. I had to allow myself the permission—and the time—to grieve. As I did, so did they. My daughters didn't need a hero. They needed their dad, the one who was mortal and human and hurt . . . who suffered heartaches like their own.

Healing is a process that begins with hurting. If you never fully hurt, you never fully heal. My three little girls, adorned in Marianne's jewelry, taught me how to be honest about my pain, which is all they needed me to be.

CHAPTER THREE

A Brooding Storm

There's blood in the sky

painted on the horizon

a withered hand stretched

a wounded heart emptying

standing in position too weak

waiting in line again with a doubtful smile,

as warm as the sun,

as dark as the night,

as lost as a stranger;

you touched them all.

I'm standing on this side of time waiting

with a hand open,

a heart yearning.

You lead me to greener fields, cooler waters.

There is no more want, no more waves.

THE GOSPEL WRITERS describe an encounter between Jesus and a woman with an uncontrollable bleeding problem. Doctors couldn't find a cure. Each attempt had failed, and no medical options remained. I imagine the woman's heart sank a bit lower every day, with each drop of lost blood. She could have resigned herself to ride out the storm and hope for the best. Her problem was out of her control, unmanageable by all known treatments. But she made one final, desperate attempt for healing.

"Who touched me?" Jesus asked.

As He walked down the road, surrounded by grasping hands and lonely hearts, He felt one hand in the midst of many. One lone hand, sensing an available opportunity, had gotten close enough to make contact with the hem of His cloak.

With the commotion surrounding Him and all the hands reaching and grasping, it was as if time stood still. Jesus stopped, looked around, and found her. In that beautiful moment of exposure and vulnerability, Jesus looked into her tired eyes.

I like to think the interaction between the woman and Jesus went something like this:

"I'm sorry. I didn't know what else to do. I have tried so many other things that didn't work. I didn't mean to interrupt. I just thought . . ."

"I came here just for you."

"What?"

"You need more than an end to the bleeding. Your heart is lonely and searching. You need healing, but your heart is wilting without answers. And that's why I am here."

In those moments, the noise of the crowd vanished. It was just the woman and Jesus. After she experienced the warmth of His smile and the power of His touch, time began again. The noise of the crowd returned as she stood healed, but more importantly, whole.

Her disease was gone, and her heart was filled. Eternity found her as she stumbled about in the dust, bloody and darkened by a life that was confusing and terrifying. The crowd and commotion moved on with Jesus as she stood there, alone but no longer lonely. He had found her.

There is a tension in our hearts, a gravity between earth and sky. It's a void between what we feel and what we want, a longing between what we believe and what we trust.

In this tension between earth and sky, God meets us. It is here where human frailty meets faith, where our hearts need to be found and healed. The moments when earth meet sky in our lives usually occur when we are most vulnerable—out of answers and explanations, and in need of something bigger. Those are moments that define us . . . or rather, redefine us.

• • • • •

Marianne was diagnosed with epilepsy when she was a young child. For years she struggled to make sense of why she continued to have problems. She wondered when God would heal her.

Throughout her life, she carried the weight of unanswered prayer, of God's inactivity. It was a dark part of her heart where she was vulnerable and weak, where earth definitively met sky.

Marianne's diagnosis was her secret . . . something she didn't want others to know. Most of her seizure activity came in the form of petit mal seizures, but from time to time, she also had more intense grand mal seizures. Her disease was unpredictable, uncontrollable, and at times, barely manageable. She was embarrassed by it.

Grand mal seizures are violent and dramatic, but the smaller, petit mal seizures are quick and often unnoticeable. Most of the time, her petit mal seizures didn't affect her daily life. Her eyes would momentarily flutter, causing her to hesitate for a second or two. She described it as "zoning out." She would lose consciousness for tiny fractions of time then continue a conversation and regular tasks at a normal pace. Though her seizures might go unnoticed by others, she was acutely aware of each one.

When we first met, I had no idea there was anything different about Marianne. She was beautiful and intelligent and full of life. In fact, I couldn't detect *anything* wrong with her. She seemed so well put together and defined by her passions. She captivated me. It was only after we began dating that she told me about the disease she considered her tragic flaw: epilepsy.

She didn't want to tell me but knew she had to. I remember the phone ringing. We talked for a bit, but her words seemed distracted and hesitant.

"Um, I have something I feel I have to tell you. Something you should know about me if we're going to keep dating."

We hadn't been dating long at that point, but we were serious enough in our relationship to know we were certainly headed somewhere together. We both shared the feeling that this could be it. *We could be it.* The message was unspoken, but we sensed it clearly.

"Okay, what is it?"

I wasn't yet clued in to the serious tone of her voice.

After a few minutes Marianne's words began to hover and stall. "I don't really know how to say this. I hope you don't think any differently about me."

As I heard her struggle to express herself, I finally realized she was having great difficulty. "Marianne, seriously, what is it? Just tell me."

"I have seizures. I have epilepsy." She went on to tell me she didn't always know when they would happen, but they occurred regularly, every day. She told me, somewhat embarrassed, that she took medication for it.

"You've probably already guessed. That's why I occasionally zone out in our conversations. That's why it looks like I roll my eyes at times."

Apparently, she didn't know me well enough yet. Details get past me sometimes . . . actually, most of the time.

Since we had been dating, I hadn't noticed a thing. Each time we talked, the sun was shining brightly, birds were chirping beautifully, and all was well in my world. How she expected me to notice something as small and discreet as flickers of the eye is beyond me.

I had no idea she zoned out in our conversations. I was too wrapped up in the beauty that was becoming "us."

She has always carried the burden of epilepsy. Even in the most beautiful times of her life, when everything seemed weightless and free, the disease lurked in her thoughts, threatening to diminish her joy.

. . . . .

"Hello, my name is Guy Delcambre . . ."

Fear is an emotion we all experience. Growing up, I was an introverted kid who would much rather be part of the crowd than stand out. So I still have no idea what inspired me to schedule a public speaking class. Maybe I instinctively knew that enough exposure to my source of fear would lessen it. More likely, it was the fact that the teacher was the head football coach, and I had heard that he often showed movies in class.

But I had heart palpitations when I showed up, especially after he told us that our first project was to write a speech introducing ourselves and describing our lives to the rest of the class. All I wanted to do was run! And from that point, every time the bell rang to begin class, I was terrified. It had the same effect on me as a death siren or the eerie, creaking sound of a closing prison door.

Trying to avoid my gripping anxiety, I put off the first project as long as I could. The night before it was due, I realized avoidance was no longer possible. Surprisingly, I wrote the speech in a short time . . . but writing was never the issue. My terror was wrapped up in delivering the speech in front of all my extroverted classmates, who actually seemed excited to present their speeches.

When it was my turn to speak, I walked to the front of the class and stood behind the podium. I could feel the blood race through my body and press against my cheeks. Everything was hot. Sweat poured out of every pore. I was completely alone.

For a second, I stood frozen. I tried to will away reality.

"Uh, whenever you're ready there, Mr. Delcambre," the teacher said with a thick accent. He also had a sense of sarcasm, "Hopefully, that's now!"

I stared at my notes, forcing my mind to read the first word, and then it happened. I blacked out. Not in the sense of passing out and hitting the floor, but I made it through the ninety-second speech without recalling anything about it.

I once heard that whenever a person experiences tremendous, overwhelming pain, the body directs endorphins to that part of the body as a means of easing the suffering. I'm not sure if the same holds true for emotions of fear. Maybe it was just adrenaline that got me through my speech that day—similar to when an athlete is able to push through agony to perform on the playing field. Whatever happened in my brain and body, I pushed passed the fear for at least ninety seconds.

"Atta' boy! Good job, Delcambre. It wasn't terrible."

Those were the first words I remember hearing since I'd heard my voice sound out the opening of my speech: "Hello, my name is Guy Delcambre."

I discovered that fear is like the bully on the playground who is bigger than the rest of the kids because he's been in third grade before. He appears tough, but he never fights fair because he's insecure and empty. In a similar way, the threats of fear are often much worse than the fear itself. It's defeated when you see it for what it really is: a loud, obnoxious bully that's only as strong as you let it be.

Conceptually, this makes sense. But when you're standing on the receiving end of a bully, petrified with fear, concepts quickly melt like wax.

Fear provides the opportunity to trust what we can't see. We cling to what we know. As fear tries to draw our hearts captive and marginalize faith, faith responds by riveting our hearts on bigger, deeper truths. It gives us the courage to take one more step.

As a child, I was completely different from my dad in physical stature and confidence. I was small and skinny, but my growth curve suggested that I would someday be bigger than my dad. I also lacked the confidence that oozed from my dad, so maybe one day that would change, too.

My dad was scrappy and tough. He never backed down from a threatening situation. In my difficult moments, I always hoped someone else would intervene and shoulder the weight for me. My dad once told me, "Don't ever walk away from a bully. If you do, he'll just keep coming back." I always hoped I could befriend the bully and avoid the whole misunderstanding, but bullies and fear don't work that way. They don't want to make friends. They only want to make war.

Fear gives us the chance to meet ourselves in a way that we don't—and can't—when we feel safe and secure. The captain of a ship docked safely in a peaceful harbor doesn't know if his craft can withstand threatening conditions. It's only by weathering a fierce storm that he can be sure his ship is strong. In the same way, we find out what we're made of by going through life's stormy seas. Many of us long to stay in the harbor, but we experience life, hope, courage, and strength on the open water. That's where we face our fears. That's where I first began to find myself.

· · · · ·

For most kids, being afraid of the dark is an inherent part of being young, innocent, and unknowing. Things in the dark appear hidden and lurking. The same tree branch you climb during the day looks like a serial killer trying to break into your house at night! A gentle breeze animates the shirt hanging from your closet door, creating a monster who wants to harm you. So you take cover under the blankets.

It's interesting how both fear and faith come easily to a child not yet exposed to a world of logic. Too often, as we work to reduce our fears, we lose faith as well. Information—adult explanations that make sense—tend to diminish wonder. Psychologists know this, which is why they use a technique called *flooding,* which exposes the person to whatever triggers the fear.

The goal of flooding is to condition a person to adjust to and tolerate the source of fear, significantly reducing the power of the fear. The idea is that increased exposure to a trigger reduces it to a manageable level. The more a person is exposed to the source of fear, the more comfortable he becomes with it . . . supposedly.

This hasn't always been the case in my experience.

I remember one morning after Marianne and I had been dating a short while. We were just getting to know the little details, habits, and intricacies about each other. Two college friends and I had moved into an apartment across from Marianne and three of her friends. It was early on a Saturday when I heard a frantic knock on the bedroom window of my apartment. I was lying in bed, still more asleep than awake, and I remember thinking, *Wow! That must be a huge bird!*

The banging let up, and I heard Marianne's roommate Casey call my name.

"Guy! Guy! You need to come over to our apartment . . . now!"

I jumped out of bed and rushed to see what was wrong. Casey told me that Marianne must have had a seizure. She knew that something was really wrong.

I mumbled, "A seizure? What do you mean? How? Why?"

We ran across the parking lot, my heart pounding. My mind was still fuzzy. I had no idea what I would do when I got to her apartment. Casey kept talking, but I wasn't listening. I was growing more fearful with each stride. Sweat began to pour down my face as I realized the seriousness of the situation.

I struggled to think of an appropriate response. *Something must be terribly wrong. People don't just have seizures,* I thought. My only previous experience with seizures was when my brother had experienced a few as a leukemia patient. I was much younger and didn't remember much about his illness. I had only a few lasting memories about my brother Colby: repeated trips to St. Jude's in Memphis, playing with our Star Wars figurines in our bedroom closet, and playing in the backyard on a wood stack. And I have one final memory: standing next to the hearse as pallbearers loaded his casket. My dad's heavy, able hand rested on my chest while I stood as tall as I could in front of him. I was five years old and didn't fully understand why I was crying, but I remember a deep loss settled in my heart that day.

We raced to the girls' apartment. As I stood at the foot of Marianne's bed, everything was quiet and still. Her chest was moving up and down slowly, so I knew she was breathing. Her face was relaxed, but she looked disturbed, like a person who has had a bad dream. Casey told me that she had called Marianne's mom, Marie, who was already on her way. Marie had told Casey to keep the apartment quiet and let Marianne rest. She would be right over.

I knelt at the side of this beautiful girl whom I was just beginning to know, my heart beating fast from running and from the fear of not knowing if she would be okay. Then, she opened her eyes with a startled look, like she was seeing us for the first time. That was encouraging, but things hadn't completely righted themselves. Her body started to tighten as she tried to get out of bed.

I told her, "Marianne, I think you need to stay still. You've had a seizure. I'm here and Casey's here. Your mom is on her way. Are you okay? Can I get you anything? Today's Saturday, by the way." I remember the words because they just poured out of me with the nervousness of someone who felt totally out of place and insecure.

She lay back in her bed with a more natural look on her face. By now she was fully alert. "You're here? Yeah, I'm okay," she said, her voice brimming with embarrassment and apology.

"Of course I'm here. And don't be sorry about it." I tried to ease her mind. I could tell this wasn't her first seizure and probably wouldn't be her last. And in a strange way, knowing this made me feel more connected to her, like we had traveled somewhere deep and dark together. I could tell she felt the same way. Her smile said it all. It was apologetic, vulnerable, and thankful.

The fear that flooded my heart quickly subsided. However, I realized I would feel that fear many times in the years to come. Like the tide in a storm, it would swell with each seizure, but recede each time Marianne opened her eyes. Every time she opened her eyes again, my heart feared less and I trusted more that she, and we, would be okay.

While it's true that flooding—being exposed to factors that stimulate fear—may reduce our reaction, I sensed that there must be something bigger, something more prevalent, something of greater value that actually overcomes and dwarfs fear. In the years ahead, I found the Something that was always present and familiar, but never truly known.

· · · · ·

Some fears vanish as we grow up. Most adults learn to dismiss the scratching at the bedroom window at night as simply a branch moving in the wind. The only thing frightening in the corner of the bedroom is the pile of dirty clothes that needs to be picked up in the morning.

Admittedly, there are times I still rush to lock the door on dark, quiet nights when I've heard a noise outside. My heart beats faster for a moment and my breaths grow noticeably quicker at the thought of something (or someone) lurking in the darkness. But at least I can take some sort of action—to investigate, to grab a defensive weapon, or to turn on the lights.

But other fears never go away. They only get worse. They are so big, so real, and so scary that they find you no matter how old you are or how good life gets.

The worst fears are the ones you can't control. They force you to find something greater . . . or to pray that something greater will find you.

That fear invaded my life when Marianne left our family broken apart.

One of our greatest desires as a married couple had been to start a family. Yet before Marianne and I rushed into having children, we agreed to take the first three years of our marriage and explore life together. We absolutely loved each other's company and wanted to learn to live together, love each other better, and enjoy one another more. Children would come eventually, and we anticipated a family with great excitement, but the first three years would be ours.

Those were the best three years. We were young and eager. Our hearts were full of each other. I remember getting lost in conversations with Marianne and learning to see the world through her eyes. It was hard to believe that this was real, that this was actually our life. I had no idea marriage could be so real, so fulfilling, and so amazing. It literally felt like time with Marianne was God's gift to me.

The joy between us and in us was tangible. And then, it got so much better.

One of the most emotional days of my life was when Marianne told me she was pregnant with our first child. Immediately, I smiled. We were three years into our marriage. Several people had warned us marriage would be good, but undoubtedly bumpy at times. Ours had been as smooth as glass—not from lack of problems that might interfere with our happiness, but in spite of such disruptive influences. We loved being together and approached everything in unison.

Adding a child only amplified the joy we felt. Our anticipation and excitement grew as we imagined life with our new addition. It made so much sense.

Elizabeth Marie entered the world, *our* world, to so much love and happiness. I couldn't stop smiling and crying. The joy was overwhelming—the same joy and emotion that would be repeated when we welcomed Emily Anne and Chloe Grace into our lives. What we didn't know yet, however, was that we were in store for some stormy waters.

Some storms have a way of arriving suddenly. When a hurricane is miles out in the ocean, the first signs often seem insignificant. You don't notice the wind change, and you can easily mistake calm skies for the promise of beautiful weather—or in our lives, the promise of happiness and peace.

And why should we notice? It would be foolish to spend all our time sitting on the shore, looking for dark clouds. Being a pessimist, waiting fearfully for the inevitability of something bad to happen, is no way to live. We have too much to live for, too many happy moments, warm memories, and grounding conversations with those we love. Life is about living, not dying.

And yet, hurricanes can be deceptive. Gentle breezes and sunny skies make us think the day will be beautiful. Then, suddenly, terrifying winds and rain threaten everything in their path.

Shortly after we returned home from the hospital with Elizabeth, our overwhelming happiness was eclipsed by Marianne's first grand mal seizure in years. With that event, the winds changed. Like a violent tornado dropping from dark clouds, her seizure was sudden and left us shaken and confused.

Elizabeth's birth should have been the happiest time of our lives, but Marianne's epilepsy became worse and less controllable during that period. Ironically, she was more prone to seizures during childbirth. Seizures became an inevitable part of the process of bringing new life into the world.

It was bittersweet and biting.

The seizure medication that had been effective before having children became useless. Nothing worked. Marianne's seizures unearthed core insecurities and struggles in her bruised heart as she grappled again and again with why God didn't answer her prayers.

"Why won't God heal me?" she would often ask, frustrated.

This brooding storm also revealed my own insecurities, which had remained quiet and undisturbed during our times of happiness. Loss of control has always been a great fear of mine. Marianne's disease and my inability to improve our circumstances threatened my family and our tomorrow. My fear became palpable.

Ironically, Marianne's vulnerability made her even more beautiful. It was as though what made her weak and wounded actually made her more complete, more aware, and more alive.

CHAPTER FOUR

Two Hearts, Melting Like Wax

A burning candle near wick's end,
and what do you say in the dark of night that could possibly
set the day right
and who are you that you would see the candle burning
thinly?
How are you?
Where are you?
Why are you?

EVERYTHING ENDED AS IT BEGAN.

It was a rapturous ending, fitting indeed.

We walked into the church, all holding hands as if not to lose one another. My daughters' steps matched my own. They didn't run ahead or lag behind. We were together, but smaller. The whole ritual of entering church felt a bit diminished because our family was missing someone now.

Our hearts each had a gaping hole filled with memories in the place where life was once—so recently, so lovingly, so strongly. And nothing could fill that sort of gap, not even the sweetest memories. Actually, it was hard to capture a purely sweet memory. The pleasurable memories that crossed my mind and filled my heart always felt bittersweet—and in that moment as we entered the church without my wife, maybe more bitter than sweet.

I thought of each of our daughters when they were born, how Marianne knew just how to love them. She always had the words that soothed and comforted them. I had none that day. In some ways, I had always felt second best to Marianne in our daughters' eyes, but I never felt any resentment. She was so good at loving them, and they loved how she loved them. I have always been active in leading our family, but love flowed through Marianne and showered down on our daughters' lives like a natural waterfall.

I loved how Marianne infused her life into them. But now it was only me walking with them. I kept cycling through deep emotions of anger, betrayal, loneliness, and fear. This couldn't be right. This couldn't possibly be happening. Surely I would wake up at any moment and return to the life I had known and loved. Instead, I was getting closer and closer to one ending and another beginning—of a new life neither chosen nor wanted.

As we followed Marianne's casket into the church, I felt my daughters' little hands, clammy and strong with a desperate grip. Their cheeks pressed against me, warmed by tears of loneliness. I was saddened deeply . . . grieving that their time with her had been so short and had ended so quickly. It broke my heart over and over again like a mallet smashing an endless row of mirrors.

It was almost unbearable to look into their eyes each time I assured them I loved them and everything would be okay. They were trying to understand, trying to hold on, trying their hardest not to break down in front of a dad they had never seen display such weakness. At the same time, the smallest glow of life burned in my heart. Somehow, I was thankful. And this thankfulness kept restoring my breaking heart. I knew our daughters could have had no better start in life. In a way all her own, Marianne had helped to prepare each of us for this curve in the path, the detour from all we had known and loved.

· · · · ·

Grief is the result of losing something you value. It's especially severe when that loss is someone deeply loved. A permanent hole forms right in the middle of all that you know.

But grief isn't limited to death. We feel it when we lose a job, receive a diagnosis of terminal illness, go through divorce, or experience any other significant loss. Sometimes those losses are temporary, but other losses are irretrievable. Questions linger, and all answers are unsatisfying.

Grief is a winding, treacherous path where steps are retraced in search of answers, and where we struggle to find the resolve to keep going.

To understand my loss is to know the love that was gone: Marianne.

And that's this story, a colliding of grace with grief, and of love overcoming the sinking, lonely depth of loss.

"I hold it true, whate'er befall;
I feel it, when I sorrow most;
'Tis better to have loved and lost
Than never to have loved at all."
—Alfred Lord Tennyson

. . . . .

We walked down the aisle of the church, my three daughters and I, through a sea of faces stained with tears. We felt the crowd's love and deep sympathy and, I suspect, their pity. I know I would have felt pity if I had been a loving observer. When we got to the front, we took our seats. Everything faded in my mind for a second, except for one remaining thought, *How did we get here, to such a sudden, unexpected end of a remarkable life that was building all around us?*

My mind drifted back in time in search for answers . . .

It was a cool, crisp spring morning when I was still young and directionless. The day felt energized with life and activity as I stood on the college campus beneath trees that blossomed and stretched in the warmth of the sun. That's when I saw the most beautiful sight. This girl not only distracted me from the mundane start to my day; she demanded my attention and my wonder. She was beautiful beyond physical cues. The way she walked and carried herself was delicate and graceful, yet strong.

The morning seemed to warm even more as I watched her walk across campus. Seeing her was like experiencing a beautiful poem that envelopes and surrounds an idea with deep descriptive words and breathes life into what would normally be regular and uneventful. When I saw her, I noticed nothing else, even though countless people passed between us heading to class.

I had never witnessed beauty so simple and elegant. I didn't want that moment to end, but she was walking in a different direction to class. In my brief history and limited experience with girls, that felt just about right—the fact that we were going in opposite directions.

Typically, I wasn't the smoothest guy in relationships. I was more of a loner and a dreamer, and the thought of getting too close to anyone made me sweaty and nervous. I preferred skateboarding with people I didn't have to know very well. I felt much more comfortable being *around* people than being in relationships *with* people. I wondered if I would ever have real, meaningful relationships.

I knew a lot of people, but I didn't let them know me. I had a few close friends, and if they weren't around, I felt lost. I avoided feeling vulnerable at all costs. Meeting someone new was a crazy, risky undertaking.

I didn't date much when I was growing up. Even in college, I hardly dated at all. Girls made me nervous—not in general, just in terms of having to put myself out there. The immediate fear that outweighed the initial prospect of liking a girl was that I was pretty sure my interest wouldn't be reciprocated.

And the sting of rejection, well, *stings*. It was simpler to withdraw and stay hidden. But I didn't realize what this approach was doing to my life and my expectations. By withdrawing, I was disqualifying myself from my dreams.

As time passed, my world got smaller and heavier. Instead of things working out, I worked harder to protect myself from failure and to prove myself. Life was moving faster than I wanted to go. Everyone else seemed to be doing just fine, building relationships, being themselves, unhindered and happy. Meanwhile, I fell aimlessly into each day, hoping that life would somehow unfold into something meaningful. I lived half awake, wanting life, but doubtful I would find it.

Then, she appeared. When I saw her on campus that spring morning I wanted to reach farther and risk more . . . and I didn't even know her name.

That semester moved along much like the one before, except she was there. Her existence made life exceptional. It was as though she had stepped off of another planet. She didn't fit into the world I knew. She was vivid with radiant color while everything else was monochromatic. Her movements were full of grace. The way she walked and stood out in the mundane background captured my mind. I began to notice only her. All day, every day, I thought about her and wondered what she was really like.

"Could she really be that good . . . as good as I imagined?"

This girl was different from others. She was beautiful in so many ways. Even as a casual onlooker, I noticed her beauty when she looked warmly at people and gave them genuine attention, when she spoke with compassionate words, when people loved to be with her. She was so attractive.

All too often, though, she was in a crowd surrounded by friends, which made it difficult for me to get to know her. I had no idea how to introduce myself.

After only a short time, I resigned her to a dream perfect for someone other than me . . .

"Marianne Rosin."

"What? Who is that?"

"That's her name . . . the girl on campus. You know . . . the one you asked about."

My roommate, Shawn, was my polar opposite. We were both from Louisiana and had met before we started college. We decided it made sense to room together. He had a thick, unmistakable Cajun accent that people in Texas loved to hear, not to mention a great, inspiring vibe. People loved to be around him.

Since we were roommates and hung out together, people often assumed I was cool like Shawn. I had no accent and could have been from the Midwest for all anyone knew. But my connection to Shawn was like a social facelift. He knew everyone on campus, or actually, everyone on campus claimed to know him.

We went to Southwestern Assemblies of God University with about 1,300 other students. It wasn't a big campus, smaller than many high schools in fact, but that was part of what made it such a great environment. Most students were there for the specific purpose of discovering and exploring God's unfolding direction in their lives. In that way, Southwestern felt like a laboratory where students experimented and developed aspects of faith. And despite the small student population, it was still easy to get lost in the social circles.

Shawn had a magnetic personality that transcended the neatly drawn circles of relationships. Naturally, he knew Marianne. His connections, though, didn't help me. I still hadn't gotten to know her.

A year went by, and I was still shuffling along, not really sure what I was doing. Everyone else seemed to know exactly where they were headed in life. It seemed that school was merely a formality for them—the kickoff party for the amazing life they were preparing to live. This was obvious by the apparent ease with which they walked through each day.

Marianne was one of these people—gliding through life, floating gloriously to some great future. The more I watched her, the more it was obvious to me that someone was going to be a lucky guy . . . but I always pictured *some other* guy.

Life was sliding through my hands like fine grains of sand. I didn't know what I was going to do in life.

Then, one day the stars aligned perfectly.

I was sitting in the Regency, a building on campus that housed a bookstore, student mailboxes, a café, and various offices and classrooms. Students tended to hang out in the Regency between classes.

The new spring semester was just beginning. It had been a year since the first time I saw Marianne. Our paths had come close several times during that year. We shared a couple of the same friends, but we had never even had a conversation. All I knew about her was what I had heard in passing conversations, but that was about to change in the slightest, but most decisive way.

Shawn and I were caught up in an important discussion about our new classes. Undoubtedly, our conversation centered on getting out of as much classwork as possible—you know, the stuff that really matters to a college student and a quality education. At least, my part of the conversation did.

Our directionless meandering about classes was suddenly interrupted when Marianne casually walked up and said hi. She was trying to drop a class, but she was undecided on what to schedule in its place. My roommate had the answer. "You definitely should schedule archery! Besides, Guy and I are in the class."

As I listened, nodding and smiling in agreement, I wasn't sure that would be enough to sell her on it. After all, she didn't exactly know us or hang out with us. But I tried to persuade her to spend more time in my presence. I asked, "How much easier of a class can you get?"

She grinned radiantly and agreed, "Yeah, that sounds fun!"

I was amazed at myself for contributing something. This girl brought out the best in me. All I wanted was to know her.

Marianne signed up for the class. Every Monday and Wednesday we spent time together in class shooting arrows at a target with different types of bows. (The whole time, I was aiming at a completely different target.) I loved seeing her laugh and crack jokes. She was incredibly witty and funny. As the semester went on, our friendship grew. We even began to meet on campus and hang out. We continued conversations started in archery class and joked about how we weren't even remotely good at archery. Surely, we were missing the point. After all, at some crucial time in our lives and careers, we would certainly need to lean on our archery skills, right?

Our teacher was the football coach, and I'm positive he had rarely, if ever, touched a bow before he began "teaching" archery.

Toward the end of the semester, he announced that our final grade would be determined by, what else, shooting arrows at a target. One thing he said captivated me. "If you hit a bull's-eye, you get an automatic A and can be done with the class early."

I looked at Shawn and Marianne, and said with the conviction of a prodigious archery master, "Done." They, of course, laughed it off, and they were right. None of us had even been close to the bull's-eye that semester. Instead, we would shoot with our eyes closed, holding the bow with our non-dominant hand, and whatever else we could think of to make our time more fun and interesting.

At the final shooting, I was the first to grab the bow and step forward. I took aim, steadied my arm, slowed my breathing, and calmly released the arrow.

And my life, for one instant, became a movie in which I was the starring hero.

Bull's-eye! First shot. Shawn and Marianne just stood there, mostly in disbelief.

I can assure you that skill had nothing to do with it. The grade had nothing to do with it. Instead, it was a determination to be done with the class and relax in my dorm room. That's what helped me accomplish the unthinkable.

To say I wasn't shocked would be an outright lie, but how cool is it to call a shot and make it? Success in that way, with that sort of confidence, was abnormal for me. I was definitely going to revel in the glory of the moment by walking out on top. I nodded at the coach and exited the class.

Marianne didn't have the same success. I ran into her the next day near the cafeteria, and she mentioned that she had to return to the class in order to complete the final.

She smiled and joked about my miracle shot.

I asserted that I could definitely make the shot again. With that shot I had entered the ranks of an elite few, like Robin Hood. I casually offered to help her when she returned to complete her final later in the day, an offer that opened the door of our friendship even wider.

From that day, our friendship quickly grew strong and familiar. It was as if I had always known her—her smile, her eyes, and the way they looked into me.

Words couldn't come fast enough when we were together. They lodged in our hearts, pulling us together like thread stitching two pieces of fabric. Time together was magical, and it seemed we had a lot of time to give each other.

We had unexpectedly stumbled upon a deep and connected feeling in our hearts, as if a connection had always been there, lying dormant. I loved Marianne almost instantly.

I felt truly alive for the first time. Unlike most previous friendships, I felt no fear of failing in this relationship. Still, to be honest, I was surprised that we were dating. I always thought she could do better, but being together felt natural and right.

We got lost in conversations about life. As in any relationship, we learned more about each other. We discovered what we liked, what we wanted out of life, and what we expected to find in the days ahead. The more we shared words and time, the more the context of our future began to merge and fit together. We began to dream in common, and the future began to include us both . . . *together.*

The more I learned about Marianne, the more I discovered about myself and who I could be without fear.

She was unspeakably important to me and the person I was becoming.

．．．．．

My mind suddenly returned to the events in the church. Memories of joyful days in the past yielded to the present emptiness and the frightening future. In the reality of sitting with my daughters at my wife's funeral, the collision occurred—worlds pushed against one another. They couldn't both exist. One would be lost. Either grief and loss would redefine us, or grace and love would memorialize the past into strength for every day ahead.

Grief is a process that leads through tossing seas and turbulent times. Eventually, waters calm and skies clear, swallowed in the morning light of a new day. I think it's true that grief is a lifelong companion as you walk the path that begins at the end of what was familiar and leads to a time when your hands learn to hold life again.

Grief reminds us that life is fragile and all is good, even when good is lost. I stood without Marianne in the church that day, feeling little hands reach for mine . . . and it was good. Even then the sense of well-being glimmered softly with the luminance of a small candle flickering defiantly in the storm. The glow of grace and love burned through the cold of death, and it was getting good.

After the agony of losing a loved one, after the helplessness to do anything about it, and after the emptiness that claims all the space in our hearts, a new day awaits. Night lingers longer than we wish, and cold permeates deep to the bone, but dawn will come again just as promised. Sooner or later, God's grace and love find us again. God searches the deep, lifting those who are sinking.

I stood alone. But after years of knowing and loving her—and even more, being shaped by her—I was ready to live beyond her role in my life.

Julian of Norwich knowingly spoke of God who owns dawning days and captures aging night: "All shall be well, and all shall be well and all manner of thing shall be well."

CHAPTER FIVE

A Porch, Two Rocking Chairs, and a Setting Sun

There is a house that I've never visited, but it always remained ahead of me on the path I was traveling. I don't know what it really looks like. I've never physically been there, but it exists in my heart. I imagine it to be small and open, tucked away in a mountain pass and surrounded by tall, sheltering trees, hidden from the chaos of life and everything trying to threaten us. It's a retreat and a refuge, a place created for me when I needed to know how to love.

I prayed for a sign once—a sign of whatever kind— to help me be sure of my way, and a vision of the house appeared in my heart. I saw a porch with two rocking chairs, warmed by a setting sun. The image spoke of forever to me and brought a sense of confidence deep in my heart.

The idea of the house feels like a dream now, but it holds a weight strong enough to center me and keep me on the path into the unknown. The image encourages me in a sure direction.

It's a beautiful house, so I love to revisit it. A stream runs completely around it, producing the most calming sound. The path leading up to its door ends at the stream and resumes on the other side. Though the waters run strong at times, strong enough to carry you away in the current, it's not a barrier to the house. Walking through the water as you approach or as you depart is an invitation to be clean and to be whole and to forget the pains, mistakes, and struggles.

A wood-burning fireplace in the middle of the house constantly warms all who are inside. It's the warmth of a love that's not perfect, but pure—the most sincere and genuine of love. The smoke that rises out of the stone chimney is a thankful offering. From the windows, a glow emits warmth, shining into the unknown. The light that escapes the panes is revealing, but easy and soft, not like a spotlight that forcefully cuts into the darkness, but like a candle that quietly but surely swallows the darkness around it.

The house isn't heavy on the land. It looks like it belongs to the earth.

I don't live there, but in a way, I exist in this house. I know that it's out there somewhere, not to be found, but to be remembered. I found it once before. That was all I needed, to be found with the one I chose to love and who chose to love me.

AFTER ONLY A FEW MONTHS of dating, Marianne and I both sensed we had something special. We really wanted to be together, but we also knew that wanting to be together is not always enough. We came from families that were very different, but in one way they were the same: broken. Because of this, we realized that love is only as solid as its foundation—the commitment to love and be loved no matter what.

It's one thing to love a person you care about because you enjoy how he or she makes you feel. It's a whole different thing to love a person on purpose . . . forever . . . each day. True love requires sacrifice, giving, and selflessness. If you love someone only for the feelings you get, those feelings are often unstable and misleading.

Love based on feelings grows shallow roots and quickly withers in times of stress. That's why two spouses can wake up one day and suddenly feel they're no longer in love with each other. Loving a person on purpose, forever, each day may feel more mechanical and less romantic, but it's so much more substantial and robust . . . and lasting.

Building a loving relationship is like building a house. You start with a vision and certain expectations. Almost immediately you envision a beautiful, comfortable house, warm and inviting. The idea of owning your own home is intoxicating. You imagine walking up to a freshly manicured lawn, smelling the fragrances of the landscaped flowers, and receiving the compliments of neighbors who admire your home and garden. But all of that is just the planning stage! The framing hasn't gone up yet; the foundation hasn't even been dug; you're still working out the budget and financing . . . yet nothing can stop you from dreaming about what it's going to look like!

Loving a person on purpose, forever, each day is a process that evolves from a *choice* to love to a *commitment* to love, no matter what. Love isn't automatic and won't develop on its own. It must be nurtured. Love seems to grow once you get beyond the idea of being in love. Only after your choice to love is tested will your commitment have the opportunity to strengthen into authentic love.

I will always look back with deep gratitude. Behind me, the love we discovered and shared glows in the distance and is preserved ever in bloom. Even now, without Marianne, our love carries through the day and into tomorrow because it was more than just her, or just me, or even both of us together. It was about a discovery, being found and holding each other tightly.

All couples face choices. Each day presents the opportunity to give up, to walk away, to become self-absorbed, and to let go. But when you find something more valuable and worthy than all else in life, you simply and forcefully refuse to let go. You hold what is precious longer.

That's what we did well. We didn't let go.

· · · · ·

Marianne's mom and dad divorced when she was young. A fragmented family was all she knew while growing up. She lived in Texas with her mom, Marie, and her two older brothers, Charles and Jimmy. Her dad, Jim, lived in another state. Marianne and her brothers often spent the better part of the summer at Cape Cod and New York with their dad and his family.

Marianne loved Cape Cod. She had fond memories and plenty of pictures of days on the beach with her dad. Her smile, the pictures show, is warm and full of life, as if life were complete for her at that moment. When she told me stories of her summers with her dad, that same smile would fill her face. The summers with her dad were life-giving gems. The last visit she made with her brothers was the summer before we were married. While she was there, we talked on the phone. Her voice was so full of happiness. We always planned to visit there some day, and I hate that the day never came for us.

Even though miles and time eventually separated them, Marianne's family was closely knit. She, her mother, and her brothers had lots of laughs and scars they shared together.

I often wondered if the reason her family was so close was due to over-compensation—much like when the body loses one of its senses and tries to make up for the loss by strengthening other areas. It seemed to be the case for her family.

Marianne and her mom shared a connection that was much closer than mother and daughter. Her mother was her hero who had the ability to thrive throughout tremendous difficulty while nurturing her three children. Marianne loved her mom deeply. They walked together through dark, uncharted valleys in life and stood together on mountaintops. Marie has an easy way about her, a way that flexes with life and absorbs hurt. Marianne was cut from the same cloth. It was part of her inner beauty.

Because of such natural grace, Marianne attracted those who hurt. She often got wrapped up in conversations with friends, even girls she had just met. She knew when they simply needed to be heard and accepted. She listened, absorbing and connecting with whatever was troubling them. And when appropriate, she unassumingly interjected the right words to lighten their burdens. It was a special gift. I think she got it from her mom.

Marianne's family wasn't like mine at all. Ours suffered a slow erosion, masked by smiles. Everything seemed to be stable for a long time as we clung to what had always been. But as time progressed, small cracks appeared and grew.

I knew something was off. My younger sister knew it, too.

My family separated slowly, like pulling a bandage off a wound gradually to avoid the ripping pain, only to find that the extended pain is even worse.

I thought I had grown up in a healthy family. My mom and dad loved both me and my younger sister, Andrea. They supported everything we wanted to do. My dad was my coach, which meant he was also my trainer and my hero. But then, dad was gone.

My dad and I are similar in many ways. As many had pointed out, "I am my father's son." But when he left, he chose a path wide enough only for himself, leaving behind much pain for the rest of us. That man was not the father I knew, and I didn't ever want to be like him.

Like many odd turns in life, the grief of losing my father led to some bits of good. For example, I discovered God in a very real way as I watched my mom suffer a broken heart and then learn to breathe all over again. Her strength inspired my sister and me. Quietly, she grew stronger as time moved on. For years, she hoped for reconciliation with my dad—not because she was afraid of loneliness, but because of her growing and deepening relationship with God.

Reconciliation required that my dad return as a changed man, and that never happened. But I witnessed a pure love in my mother's heart and a determination to live unhindered by bruising circumstance. She learned the secret of perseverance. From my mom I learned how to love with a full heart.

My mom is quietly consistent, always giving, and lovingly faithful. Her faith is daring and strong, weathered and nurtured by life's great storms, thriving on an arduous path she didn't choose. She has shown me not only how to survive, but also how to rebuild by mending broken pieces and putting them back in place. She isn't a victim; she's a pioneer whose example is lodged in my heart.

Marianne and I both came from broken families; we both surfaced from the depths, scarred but stronger. We absolutely didn't want to make the same bad decisions and cause similar pain. We agreed it would be better for us not to marry if we weren't sure it was God's will. We didn't want to tear a family apart. Who does? But that strong possibility awaits a love based only on emotion. More than anything, we were searching for a sign pointing to a lasting commitment.

· · · · ·

The strongest foundation of love is the commitment between two people to love each other. In order to love each other fully and without doubt, Marianne and I needed to be certain that we were supposed to choose one another. I was all in. She fit me in the most perfect ways. However, there was—for a time—something uncertain in her, and then for us both. We needed to be certain.

A tension arose in our relationship that didn't exist before. Was this a sign? How could we be sure, one way or the other? We were young, too young by the account of some people, to be so involved so quickly. The tension hung in the air in our conversations. We talked about the fact that if we weren't certain of our future together, then we should take a step back and reevaluate.

I was afraid. It was speech class all over again! Fear had found me, threatening to unravel the most beautiful thing in my life.

My first response to the fear was to give up on our relationship as suddenly as I had committed to it. My language began to change from hopeful to dreadful. The sky was falling, and all possibility of love was vanishing in the fog of fear. We agreed to completely break off communication with each other for a week to spend time in prayer. It sounds devout, but it was more desperate than pious.

Above all, we were both absolutely certain that God was our highest priority—as individuals and potentially as a couple. We wouldn't allow anything to shatter that conviction, not even our deepest emotions and desires. The risk of losing something we shouldn't have was well worth testing our relationship.

Being apart for a week wasn't difficult because it came at the end of the spring semester. I was headed home to Louisiana for summer break. I had plenty to do there. But the purposeful lack of communication and the possibility of this being the slowest, most delayed goodbye was killing me. As I drove from Dallas to my hometown of Abbeville, I was a mess. It was six hours of melting and churning emotions.

I should never have agreed to this! She's probably going to decide that we shouldn't be together. And some other guy is undoubtedly going to move in on her during the summer. She'll forget about me!

In six short hours, I allowed fear to reshape months of amazing conversations and connection. I was afraid that our week apart would drive us away from each other. Our goal wasn't to abandon the relationship, but to test if what we had was real and strong enough to build our lives on. We didn't want to repeat the path that either of our parents had taken. We wanted our hearts to be strong enough to stay together.

Reluctantly, at first, I prayed. I asked to be reconnected with Marianne. I prayed not to lose her and the future we had discussed. During our week apart, our prayers were to be for clarity, but fear laced each of my thoughts—fear of losing what seemed to be too good in the first place. Each time I paused to pray, I asked God for a definitive sign, a confidence that what we had was real. I prayed for Him to show Marianne the same thing. I prayed for a green light, a nod of approval, assuring me that I wouldn't lose her. I didn't realize it, but it was a defensive posture.

I didn't want to lose Marianne, but fear continually suggested that was what was happening. Love is something you can't hold too tightly, or you risk smothering it and choking the life out of it. Love is delicate and must be handled with care.

Love is an open hand, giving before it expects to receive. Yet I was determined to defend and protect my stake in our relationship. I absolutely could not and would not lose her. In fear, I held on much too tightly. My mind loved the *idea* of loving her, and I resisted the possibility of heartbreak if God decided, for some reason, to lead her away from me.

I was radically insecure. I still held to the thought that Marianne could do much better than marry me. In the back of my mind, I even thought she was selling herself short by choosing to be with me. I didn't want to limit the potential of her life. My fear and insecurity rushed to the surface during our week apart. It was a climactic showdown, a risk that I would lose and once again be reminded that many things were too good for me.

Honestly, I fully expected God to speak directly and clearly to Marianne about our relationship, but not to me. I had never heard God speak. If I somehow got an answer from Him, I had no idea what that answer would be like.

When people spoke of hearing from God, I had little idea what they meant. Only rarely had I ever felt something within me that might be God directing me. As I prayed that awful week, I offered up words and wished for the best, hoping that by giving space to our relationship we would verify the adage that absence makes the heart grow fonder.

Yet in my desperation and anticipating losing Marianne, God interrupted my confusing inner melodrama. He gave me a clear and powerful thought, an anchoring image that, to this day, stays vibrantly alive in my heart and mind. I saw a glimpse of us both relaxing on a porch in two rocking chairs, watching a setting sun . . . nothing else. In that moment, I saw the future. That image set everything right and removed my fear. Without doubt, I knew that Marianne was the one—the one I would choose to love and the one I knew would love me fully in return.

I knew that everything was right. Confidence swallowed fear, and that's how I knew God had placed that thought there. It was a quiet thought that surfaced in my mind as I was waking up one morning. I hadn't been praying. It was almost like the first moment you awake, when you're still half dreaming and your thoughts are blurry. The thought was new, yet it felt familiar—like it had always been in my heart.

To say that this thought was only about love and Marianne would be to diminish its importance. The image created an actual place in my heart, a house that I'm building, or is being built by God, the essence of earth and sky intersecting . . . a place founded at a time when God so precisely interrupted all that was wrong in my heart and revealed hope for me. It was the first time in my life that I felt like I was traveling with God rather than hoping to catch up to Him.

This was a house worth revisiting for the rest of my life.

CHAPTER SIX

The Darkest Day

And what of this beautiful mess,
colors melting into a still pool of sadness?
Who can know or hear the whispers sounding
a destructive cracking, carried on an enemy wind,
a stranger's glance,
a night knowing no end?
And what stares back from the darkest black,
a haunting hollow that knows me better than I know myself,
a deep earthen hunger unsatisfied within my chest?

WHEN I LOOK BACK, I see a life I hardly recognize anymore. It looks like a painting with beauty and strength apparent in each brush stroke. It makes sense, and it is undisturbed. It sits in place just as it should.

As I write this, a year has passed. Three hundred sixty-five days ago, my life looked normal, happy, and hopeful. The new school year had just begun. Elizabeth was excited about her third-grade year. She was looking forward to field trips, class parties, school projects, new friends, and award ceremonies—all the things that made her thrive.

Emily was a first-grader. Kindergarten was finished, and she was finally in a "real" grade. She couldn't wait to get the year started.

I was barely a month into a new job. With my new role came a better salary. We finally had enough of a financial cushion not to wonder how we would meet our bills each month, which enabled us to focus on new challenges and evolving dreams.

A couple years earlier, we had taken a leap of faith and moved from Louisiana to Texas as part of a leadership team starting a new church. We knew the job at the church wouldn't provide enough income because my salary only covered about two-thirds of our monthly budget. But a new door had opened, and we were finally at a more-than-stable place financially. Lots of new and really good things were happening in our lives.

Just a few days before school, Marianne planned a family shopping trip so the girls could get some new clothes. She was consistently celebrating important moments in their lives. Shopping with mom was a treat for them. While the two older girls tried on clothes and proudly modeled them for Marianne, Chloe and I sat there, bored out of our minds and wishing we were somewhere else.

Chloe wanted food.

I wanted coffee.

Chloe hopped on my back, and we went searching for anything that would rescue us from the fitting rooms. I can remember being a good distance away and still hearing Marianne's voice, "Oh, girls. *I love it!* You both look so beautiful!"

I shook my head and smiled.

That was life then, and it was truly beautiful. Never would any of us have imagined that in just a few short days, that life would be no more.

One year ago . . . things were still undisturbed. My life wasn't a picture that I saw in retrospect. It was real and immediate, happening, as it should, in the moment. The day after that shopping trip was the day things went wrong. That was the day Marianne was rushed to the ICU. That was the day we had our last conversation.

Looking back a year later, everything appeared perfectly in order. Life was full of love. It was plain in the best of ways, plain in the way that you hope for, when life is favorable and effortless.

It may seem strange—maybe even wrong—but I wouldn't trade this day for that one. I can remember and cherish that life, but it is no more. If I do anything but remember it, that life steals from this day. And that beautiful life never stole from me. It only added to me, and I will only allow it to continue to add to who I am.

I loved Marianne deeply, in a way that challenges me as a writer to fully and accurately describe it. Maybe I can at least offer some hints at the depth of love we shared.

The Day Before

It was a day so mundane that it nearly slipped into the past unnoticed. I'm not suggesting that every regular day was forgettable. All the calm and normal days were simply compiled into our story together, one where we experienced happiness, thankfulness, and satisfaction. We were on a steady course into forever. And maybe forever still wouldn't be long enough.

I woke up anticipating a good day. Typically, I was the first one awake in the house. I enjoyed the first few quiet moments of the morning alone, reading. A short while later Marianne was downstairs getting coffee, journal in hand. She was great about journaling her thoughts, prayers, struggles, and expectations. I met her in the kitchen for a second cup. We smiled, said our good mornings, and talked about something—I don't recall what—for a few minutes.

It was our routine. Neither of us was particularly good at mornings, but we both thoroughly enjoyed the quiet of the early hours before the kids were awake and the hustle of the day began. All too soon we heard the soft sound of footsteps descending the stairs, transitioning us into the day and signaling the beginning of the rest of our morning routine: breakfast, random stories about tiny details from the school day before, rushing to get dressed, protests from the girls about what they didn't want to wear, packing lunches, more coffee.

When the dust settled, we were all happy again and ready for the day. As usual, I dropped the girls off at school. Chloe and Marianne typically enjoyed the morning together in the recliner, watching cartoons. I was supposed to meet a coworker who was training me in a new hospital, but after taking the girls to school I got a call saying something had come up and he wouldn't be able to meet until later in the morning. I had an extra hour or so to stay home. As a result, Marianne and I sat in the kitchen sipping coffee and talking while Chloe watched cartoons.

It was a great morning, different from most. We lazily moved through conversation about everything and nothing at all. We enjoyed it so much that even with the extra time that morning, I found myself running late.

I kissed Marianne and Chloe, said goodbye, and ran out the door. That was the last time I looked into Marianne's eyes, and the last time she saw me. She called me at work later that morning, and we talked about dinner later that night, a dinner that never would happen.

That was the last time we spoke to one another.

Everyone says goodbye at some point. You just don't expect to do it on a random Wednesday.

I finished my work for the day an hour early, so I headed home to surprise the girls. I had been working long hours, and I didn't like the fact that getting home after six o'clock had become normal. I was glad I would be home before 5:00 for a change. Undoubtedly, the girls would continue playing with their neighborhood friends, but they would still be happy for me to be home earlier. And Marianne would certainly be glad to see me.

Just ten minutes away from our house, I received a text message from my sister. "Is everything okay with Marianne?"

"I guess so. Why?"

No response followed my return text. I figured that Marianne once again had left her phone upstairs or downstairs or wherever she wasn't. She was good at regularly losing her phone.

Five minutes later, I called Marianne's phone just to make sure all was well. It rang a few times. Then her mom answered.

Weird, I thought. And then I heard a barrage of words that invaded our world. Words like *paramedics* and *she's not responding.* Words like *Guy* and the *ER.* Those words divided the world in two: what was, and what would no longer be.

I rushed back to the hospital where paramedics were taking my wife, the one where I now worked, the one where I had trained all afternoon. I got there before them and paced uneasily for what seemed like an eternity.

Our friends Scott and Shannon were the first to arrive, displaying faces as brave as they could. That's typically when you know something is really wrong, when you detect genuine but passing pity in the face of a friend witnessing a tragedy in your life.

Fear.

Panic.

Dread.

Numbness.

I don't remember a word of consolation Scott offered. I just remember thinking how thankful I was for him to be there and that I didn't have to say anything. He would be a solid shoulder, taller and more present than most, in the week ahead. Everything around me was happening so fast. It felt like my heart was on pause.

I remember threatening a nurse who wouldn't let me see my wife: "You will buzz me through right now or I'm coming through!" Finally, I stood at the foot of Marianne's gurney. Nurses swarmed around her, saying things I didn't hear . . . things I probably didn't want to hear.

One nurse asked me, "Hey, are you okay?" Her name was Becky. For whatever reason, I instantly felt alert as I stood next to her. It was as though my heart un-paused, and I was in real time again, wading through the heaviness of crisis.

Others asked me questions about insurance and what to do if her heart stopped again. "I'm not sure . . . give me a minute . . . just a second," was my repetitive reply. I saw them resuscitate her, and everything changed again. They stabilized her condition to move her to ICU. But I already felt she was gone.

For hours, I floated between reality, memories, and what-if's. Then I realized it was the next day.

Day One

Sometimes you hear sad stories and cling to the words. The heavier the situation becomes, the more you hope distance carries away the ugliness, the unbelievable, the tragedy, the disparity of it all. It seems too overwhelming to be real or fair or bearable. And then, when you think sadness has peaked, when it seems as though the worst has come on shore and terrified everyone enough, it sinks deeper. The sadness swallows life like a black hole, causing it to disappear into nothingness with no expectation of return.

People began to call. Friends and family showed up at the hospital. As they appeared, I retracted deeper into sadness. At those times you want people near, yet you want them far away. Their presence reminds you that something is terribly amiss. Something is wrong enough to bring them there . . . and to keep them there. Yet their presence is also comforting and reassures you that, for at least that moment, you won't float away alone into a dark night.

Visitors smiled and spoke words of comfort, but their sadness was evident. I felt pity in each hug. And I felt a growing loneliness in the company of those I loved the most. Faith didn't lift me. It didn't support me. It sat precariously between one life and the other, like a collapsing wooden bridge. One life and the other; I didn't know which I was in.

When I realized I had moved into another day, I knew the crisis was real. It was as if I had woken from a daze, but in two. I felt like two people existed inside of me, like I was separating from myself. Part of me was in hiding, resisting the truth. The other part wanted to remain close to the pain and sadness because that was the only place I still felt connected to Marianne.

Hope existed in the love that connected us, but fear was consuming this hope like a mold. I was aware of everything, but my hope felt day-old. I knew where I was, I remembered what happened, and I knew I had never been this sad before. I didn't know sadness could be like this. It wasn't a sadness that cried out and wanted to escape. Rather, it wrapped tightly and coldly around my heart and stayed still. My body was tired, but I didn't want to sleep. For the most part, I couldn't. I would doze off for moments, only to wake up feeling like I had just been staring into space, not sleeping.

Everything was a bit fuzzy and people's words seemed like distant echoes. I lost a few hours that I can't seem to remember. Nothing. No recall. No recollection. Just empty, lost hours. I was floating and sinking at the same time.

My good friend John rarely left me. He smiled warmly and spoke softly. When I was sinking, his voice was one of the few I could still hear. It helped me find my way back. He doesn't know it, but I saw God in him, and it saved me. He drove me home that day, the first full day Marianne was in the hospital, so I could take a shower and gather some clothes. I didn't say much at all. He knew I was hiding. "It's okay," he kept saying. I didn't feel like everything was okay, but those words gave me courage that lasted and would reappear in my heart, although not just yet. At the time I wasn't even floating; I was taking on a lot of water.

I walked into my house for the first time in almost two days. Everything was the same as when I had left it. My mug from the morning before was still in the sink. The house looked normal, but it felt like someone else's house. I took a shower, and the only thought I remember clearly was, "I want to die." I felt like a coward, but I couldn't help it. My mind was crushing beneath the weight of it all, of her fading. I didn't want to leave my house and return to the hospital to watch her die slowly. I couldn't handle it. I just wanted to die.

But John had said he was coming back for me in ten or fifteen minutes. The next thing I remember is the drive back to the hospital. "It's gonna' be okay," John said again. This time I felt his words cut through my sadness like the smallest light in the darkest night. It set my heart on fire. I didn't feel as cold. I didn't feel as lost. I didn't want to die.

Walking back into Marianne's room, I felt as though I was at the bottom of a mountain that disappeared into the vastness of the sky. It was a long way to the top, and I wasn't sure I could make it—but I knew I had to try. I didn't know what I would find once I got there, but it was the only way to go. Staying at the bottom meant sinking and coming apart even more. I hoped I would find Marianne at the top. I hoped that her eyes would open slowly and her smile would return to her face. In the back of my mind, I knew I might never see that beautiful sight again. But I had to venture forward. I had to climb, to escape, to reach the top and see what was waiting. With each heartbeat, I felt different. In one beat, I felt like I could take it all. In the next one, I crumbled again. Again and again . . . standing and falling.

Day Two

Time was an ebbing current sluggishly carrying us away from each other, which left me wondering, waiting, and weaning. I began to spend a little less time in her room. I couldn't just sit there watching the machines hold her in this life. I felt like I was on shore but she was on a tattered raft floating with the tide, drifting away but still within an arm's reach.

That's when you're most desperate, when someone you love is still in reach, when hope still exists. Once the tide pushes you too far apart, a different kind of desperation sets in—the kind that still wants, but desires what has *been* lost, not what is *being* lost.

When I was outside her room but still nearby, hope was easier to see. It was an anchor. I felt closer to her. The sadness wasn't quite as heavy. Time moved slower and gave me the opportunity to hope.

The two people I had become were battling between life and death, hope and despair, faith and failure. Part of me was drowning in the beeping sounds, the sight of her chest inflating because of the air being forced into her lungs, the glowing, fluctuating numbers reporting her stats, the smell of death. The whole situation ripped through me with the force of a thick, dull butter knife. That part of me wanted her to die quickly and be over and done with it.

I could feel my heart ripping.

I could hear my thoughts failing.

That part of me was dying with her.

The other part of me was only getting stronger with the kind of strength that finds you in crisis—part adrenaline, part faith, part emotional suppression. When I was that person, I was clear and could hear God, but I was still afraid. I feared that faith would lift me out of loss instead of faith finding her and bringing her back to me.

I decided to leave the third floor for the first time since they had moved her from the ER to ICU. I took an elevator marked "Staff Only" so I wouldn't have to walk through the waiting area where some of the people I loved most on the planet were sitting and praying and hoping. I certainly appreciated the support, yet at times their expressions undid me. I could see sadness in their eyes.

I just had to be alone. I needed to hear something different.

As I stepped off of the elevator, tears forced their way through the walls I had erected around my heart. Nothing looked familiar. I was somewhere I shouldn't have been. Everything was labeled, "Restricted," just like my heart—isolating the crisis and containing the emotion in a controlled burn. I was lost.

I walked down hallways that seemed endless. How empty I felt.

I opened the door to a chapel and walked into a room filled with intense light. One wall was nearly all stained glass. And thankfully, the sun shining on the glass filled the room with warmth and beautiful colors that moved me out of the hospital into a different place, my heart.

I had been locked inside my head, circling in thought ever since I had called Marianne's phone and my mother-in-law had answered. Inside the chapel, the thoughts racing through my mind stopped. I didn't think about Marianne. I didn't think about death or life or tomorrow. I just sat in the warmth of light. I was awake, but I felt the ease of rest, as though I were sleeping. The amazing stillness made it seem that everything around me was frozen in place. No sounds. No people. No thoughts. Then one long sigh escaped me, carrying a thousand pounds and a thousand weighty thoughts out of my heart.

I sat there for a long time, my heart unrestricted. In the silence, God was stronger than I ever trusted He could be. I had given up looking for Him. Yet He pursued me to an unbelievable depth, one that was dark and dirty with death, but where He was still God—fully capable, completely present.

I left the chapel feeling "found." I took the regular elevator back up to the third floor, ascending out of my personal darkness back into light and life. The elevator doors opened to a room full of familiar faces. No one realized I had been gone . . . but I was back.

Then, the most beautiful thing happened. Previously, sadness had seemed the only appropriate mood, and I was in a hurry to feel it all before everything ended. Now it was as if time expanded when people offered love, support, and fond memories. The end was near, but it wasn't here yet. The two persons warring within me finally came together, in an un-ended moment, not rushing ahead in panic and not hiding in sadness. I was alive in hope, aware of what could be, yet committed to trust and love no matter what might come. I chose to bind myself to that commitment, lest I come apart again.

I felt close to Marianne no matter where I was.

Day Three

The first full day in the hospital was long. The second was even longer. This was the third.

Nearly two days remained. I was hoping for so much more.

Against impossible odds, slimmer than what reality would allow, Marianne actually had started the slightest beginning of a recovery. The doctors were able to reduce the medicine being used to keep her stable, and she seemed to be holding her own.

Every heartbeat mattered.

Every hint of a recovery seemed to make sense because of all the prayers, the promises, and the unending support from friends and strangers.

God was present.

A miracle would ensue.

Everything would be as it was.

God would be who I thought He was.

My heart swelled with faith that Marianne would awaken, and I began to say so. Rescue was apparent. Death would be subverted. God would be proven in my mind, and victory would be validated in my heart. But my faith was dictated and determined by what I wished for, not by what I knew.

For the first time in two days I left the hospital so I could clear my head and be alone. I ended up on a bench in a courtyard filled with greenery and flowers. It was peaceful. I was still very much in the violence of the storm, yet I felt at ease, mostly. I began to think and pray. I wondered if Marianne would be healed.

It would be miraculous.

I did believe.

As much as I could, I believed God for her healing. I could see tomorrow and our life resuming. We would return home deeply grateful for God's rescuing hand in her healing. Years would go by and the girls would grow. Life would go on. Milestones would be reached, dreams would be realized, and love would sink its roots even deeper.

My mind was at ease in these visions. For the first time in days, my heart was truly at rest. I trusted that the thousands praying with us had convinced God to intervene and disrupt circumstances, to interrupt tragedy and break death's grasp.

My words were strong and full. But then the quietest thought pierced my heart, almost in a friendly way. *You're going to leave the hospital alone.* It was a thought that screamed against all I had hoped and prayed for. I brushed it away, dismissing it as the residue of doubt in my heart. But it resisted and remained. It grew louder and it felt real, more than the comforting vision that had filled my head.

If this was God, I didn't believe Him.

This can't be. Why? I don't deserve this, and You can't do this to me—not to my kids, especially. You should know this!

I remember feeling grief for the first time. I also felt weak and lost.

She had seemed to be improving! Her condition had been getting better!

The doctors had been amazed. This *had* to be a miracle in the making.

Yet my heart had been pierced by trustworthy words I despised, words apparently from a God whom I thought I loved. I didn't know how to think. I just knew that I couldn't ignore or discard the thought that was louder than the rest—the one announcing defeat and loss.

What surprised me was that I wasn't angry. I felt too broken, tired, and lost. I couldn't fight anymore. I simply felt more alone than ever, and God seemed to be a million miles removed from the terror and despair that consumed my heart.

This sadness was deeper than before, when even the slimmest hope was enough to keep me from feeling completely lost. But if I had ever heard God's voice, this was it. It was clearly not from me. It was more than doubt stabbing at my heart. This was real, and I knew it.

If this is so . . . if I have to leave here alone . . . You had better come and be close to me.

I couldn't get through this on my own. Who could? It's difficult to describe the loneliness I felt. Everything was being flushed out of my heart: memories, thoughts, hopes, dreams. I was losing all that mattered. I felt nothing—not fear, not happiness, not hope or dread . . . nothing.

The chapel experience the day before seemed a lifetime ago. I wasn't coming apart like before, nor was I altogether found. Now, all of me was utterly and completely lost. I sat alone, not in the warmth of the sun, not in the company of love, not in a life where future time existed. The only thing present was the life that used to be. I was somewhere I didn't recognize: alone.

I wasn't mad at God. It was deeper than that. I wasn't fighting anymore or gripping faith so tightly. It's dark and disorienting to be lost. You have no clues where you actually are. And even though you don't recognize the location, you know it's treacherous.

I left that courtyard retracing my steps back to those who were still hoping, back to Marianne's hospital room, to the exact spot where I was losing her. I didn't feel God with me.

I just felt lost in that moment.

She was alive and apparently fighting, but I knew we would lose in the end. I didn't know how to resolve that thought. If a miracle were to happen and prove me wrong, I would be joyfully mistaken.

Her condition started to change, but for the worse. It began to hint at what I already knew.

And that is how the third day ended.

Day Four

Trust is a delicate thing, especially in the dark, when things are uncertain and unsettled, and you're exhausted. As the third day gave way to the fourth, I was tired in every way. I was sleeping now, but not deeply. I woke often during the four or five hours that I slept, and then I quickly drifted back to sleep. I could tell I was sleeping only because I kept waking up.

I didn't have the strength to pray or to think clearly. God knew what I wanted, but with each passing hour it became more apparent that I wouldn't get it. Trust was hardest during this period when it felt like Marianne definitely wasn't going to make it.

Still, I prayed and read Scripture with what little focus I had. I dwelt in a place with God I had never experienced before. I began to feel Him with me in each moment, in my weakness, in my loneliness. Higher and stronger thoughts than my own sprouted in my mind and rooted in my heart. I found an inner place that was safe from the violence of death. In that place, God was different. I wasn't searching for Him anymore; He was pursuing me. I felt His presence as sinkholes continued to collapse beneath my feet.

I wasn't connected to people at this point. It's not that I didn't want to be, I just couldn't think for longer than a few minutes. As they talked to me, I nodded and smiled, drifting in and out of focus. Many offered genuine sympathy. Friends and loved ones spoke of recovery and the possibility of healing. They prayed and I prayed—really prayed. And despite the clarity I had received in the courtyard the day before, and the growing peace and grace that resulted, I waffled back and forth between hope for a happy ending and . . . well, something else. Deep down, I knew the thought that found me in the courtyard was true, but it was hard to accept.

The doctors saw a decline in Marianne's weak and fragile condition. I saw it, too. This time my certainty went beyond pessimism or giving up. I knew that she was dying.

What about our daughters? That one question kept haunting my thoughts. Fighting, hoping, knowing, and trusting . . . the conflict in my heart and mind was messy. It was a battle I felt justified to fight, although I was more and more convinced it would be a fight to the death.

Her death. The death of my wife, my daughters' mother, the one whom I loved as completely as I knew how to love.

The night of the fourth day came quickly, and things were not promising. Her condition was much worse. I hated the thought that found me in the courtyard. I hated that God was apparently only taking care of me through this. I wanted her eyes to open just one more time so I could say goodbye. I wanted her to look into my eyes and know that I had fought, that I hadn't given up, I hadn't let go. She would know if she could just see my eyes. I know this hope was more for me than for her, but it was very real.

I was left here.

She was somewhere else where pain, sadness, and darkness do not exist.

She was fine. I knew that.

I was not. I only sort of knew that.

That night was the loneliest night I had ever lived. Nothing was happening. I went to sleep in a room the hospital staff kept open for me. I sat there hoping things would play out differently. I wasn't really thinking, just fading. I was exhausted.

It was a terrible day. The next would be worse.

Day Five

"You're blessed when you feel you've lost what is most dear to you. Only then can you be embraced by the One most dear to you."
MATTHEW 5:4, THE MESSAGE

The fifth day was the final goodbye, the letting go.

I was sleeping deeply and soundly, different from the nights before. I needed the rest and the strength. I also knew I was just waiting now, and God's grace and strength amplified in my heart that night. All was okay.

Then I heard John's voice. He woke me to tell me the nurse had said I should come now. I had slept with my shoes on, anticipating the moment with a resigned, forced readiness. Sadness filled my heart, but it felt right and no longer terrorized me.

Walking toward Marianne's room, vivid memories played in my head. I relived meeting her for the first time, seeing her radiant smile as she walked toward me down the aisle, and hearing her joyful laughter after having kids. I was strolling through past scenes in our lives . . . even as I walked toward the end of the present. It felt as though I was a step behind myself.

I arrived at her room. It felt so different now, sacred and still. I immediately sensed the transition, life and death both present. I stood beside her bedside and bent over to whisper to her, leaning around the tubes that had kept her alive. I kissed her cheek. I told her I loved her, and I thanked her.

"Thank you for a life so beautiful, for a love so real. Thank you for giving me so much more than I could have imagined."

I told her how strong I felt because of God's grace. I said I was confident that life would be rich for us still. I told her that the girls had little idea what the past week had been like for us, and that she was always so much better at talking to the girls in tough times. I was praying that the right words would find a deep place in their hearts so they would live as fully as we had always dreamed for them. I assured her that we would be okay. I kissed her cheek again and pushed my hand through her hair.

Moments later, she was gone.

• • • • •

As I write these words, Marianne died one year ago today, before sunrise, in the quiet and stillness of morning. As beautifully as she had come into my life nearly twelve years earlier, she had slipped gracefully out of it.

And there was a goodbye . . . at least, I like to think so.

I hugged her sister, whom she loved so much, and then went into the hallway. John put his arm around me and told me the nurse had detected a short but noticeable spike on Marianne's heart monitor while I was talking to her. I'm not one to make a big deal of small details that could easily be attributed to coincidence, but I will never be convinced that this was coincidence. It mattered the world to me that the nurse had noticed the change. I needed something, and I could sense God's activity even in small details. That was the first time I experienced healing after she died.

So it was, and it is.

CHAPTER SEVEN

A Crumbling Wall

DEATH IS SO BIG AND FINAL. It engulfs a person like a rising tide that swallows the shore. The days that follow can be dark, dingy, and hopeless.

I would never have guessed I could live in moments so desolate and airless.

Someone is there . . . and then she is no more. Like a moment that passes too quickly. Like an amazing spring afternoon just before the sun sinks into the horizon.

I, too, am no more. I am someone new. My identity is no longer marked by the way I live the present. I am an observer of the most beautiful memory lived in a lovely lifetime, long ago.

One world becomes lost in another. That's what the days, weeks, and months following Marianne's death felt like. I went through the motions because it made the days pass a little quicker and the darkness of night a little shorter. My answer to everyone who was concerned (or curious) was that I was okay. "As well as could be expected, I suppose."

But I was *not* okay. They knew it, and I knew they knew it.

I only claimed to be okay because this provided a safe distance from people. I didn't necessarily want to be far from everyone in my life, but I felt I had to be. My life had imploded.

The weight of loss rested heavily on my heart, producing a constant pressure. Even when I slept, I felt it.

Silence.

. . . . .

Fall slowly into night
like a blanket dripping with tears
or failure or fading,
cold cover for fire once burning steadily
and smoke rises from the smoldering mess
to clouds of silence
set on being distant.
No sounds, only the quiet now.

I didn't pray much because words couldn't express what I felt. The few times when they did, those words weren't appropriate for prayers.

To be honest, I didn't know how I felt. Beneath the pieces of my life, my heart was broken. I was lost in an awkward mix of old things familiar and new things unfamiliar.

To a large extent, the days were the same. I kept a journal of that year. At first, it was to help me remember each day and to verify that I was moving from one day to the next. It didn't feel that way. Each day was acknowledged primarily because I changed clothes and took a shower.

More than hurt or pain or loss, I was stuck, which was a bitter paradox. I still lived in the same house around the same neighbors who loved us. I still shopped in the same stores and drove on the same streets, but one thing was vividly apparent in each waking moment: my wife was no longer present. And it was difficult to hold onto her memory because it felt inappropriate even to think about her.

At every moment, I expected her to wake up, walk down the stairs, and head straight for the coffeepot. But I never heard her footsteps.

I would lower the toilet seat out of habit before remembering there was no need to bother anymore.

In such insignificant moments, I realized I had walked through a door, out of a world I had known . . . a door leading somewhere unfamiliar. By being on the other side of the door, I had left my former life.

I worried that I would forget countless things about Marianne and the life we had lived together, and I was afraid. The worry punished me each day. The memories, once so sacred, now felt cheap.

Every image in my memory moved me back to that time: smells, glances, smiles, thoughts, and moments right before or after the picture. I was losing those feelings and sensations, too.

Forgetting the treasured little details, I think, is the worst thing about losing someone you love. You remember the broad strokes of life, but how mean and wickedly cruel is grief to wipe the details away? I relished what people close to me could recall. When I heard them tell stories about Marianne, it seemed she had only taken a step backward, fading into the crowd of those who loved her. I suffered the worst blow death could finally deliver: my wife disappeared.

More hurtful than her death were the fading memories. No longer mine alone, I shared her now as a common fading memory. Family, friends, neighbors, onlookers, all stood with me as we missed her dearly. Time moved forward, pulling our existences farther apart.

After Marianne died, I remained alone. Friends called to check on me frequently, and I forged a few deep relationships that lifted me out of swelling seas of emotions and thoughts. Those friends positioned themselves in my life to keep me from drowning. They saved me, and I will be forever grateful.

But even under the caring eyes of loving friends, my loneliness lingered. When I smiled, that familiar loneliness felt stronger than any temporary feeling of happiness.

It was the past, another day, another time. And in the present, the one where I now found myself, I felt lost . . . and a little betrayed.

But I also felt close to God, in an awestruck, thoughtful way I hadn't felt since childhood.

As a kid, I once visited the French Quarter in New Orleans and saw a street performer who, for some reason, made me think about God. He was a mime in the character of a robot with movements that were odd, mechanical, and precise. Even in the sweltering heat and heavy summer air, he was painted silver from head to toe and dressed in a full suit. He never broke character for passersby. Perhaps it was his quirky, precise gestures and distinct character that caused me to think of God. Maybe it was his silence and distance from people moving around him, inviting attention but not direct interaction. Then again, it might have been the brilliance of his silver skin, suit, and hat that glowed in the stifling heat and humidity. It never affected him. For some reason, he represented what I perceived God to be.

In my youth, God seemed ambiguous, somewhere out there. It was nice to see Him perform and know where to find Him when I needed Him. But I was a bystander, not really in need of Him. My life was easy to manage, and for the most part, things usually went my way. Somehow in the end of each predicament of my young life, I usually got what I wanted or needed. And in those times when I really needed God, He came through every time, gently guiding my life. I prayed for help with my questions, and He came through with answers.

My life didn't require much interaction with God. I expected Him to be a certain way, and He was predictable. I kept my head up, my hands clean, and my words as honest as possible. God seemed happy with me, and I felt at ease.

But life doesn't always move along peaceful and undisturbed. Like the sea, which tosses angrily in one place and swells softly in another, life breaks and comes back together, sometimes pulling with confusing resolve. I suppose if life were always smooth like a glassy sea resting calm and predictable under a warming sun, God would seem more like a celestial Santa Claus or a doting grandfather. I'm not suggesting that God relies on life's ugliness and pain for validation, but the sky opens and touches our earthen souls precisely in those ripping, crippling, tumultuous moments. It's one thing to read of God dramatically saving humanity and smile casually in response. It is a completely different, powerful event when you are the one caught in the dark, swirling vortex of despair and saved from sinking.

In *A Farewell to Arms,* Ernest Hemingway accurately perceived life when he wrote:

> "The world breaks everyone and afterward many are strong in the broken places. But those that will not break it kills. It kills the very good and the very gentle and the very brave impartially. If you are none of these you can be sure it will kill you too but there will be no special hurry." [1]

After Marianne's death, my life felt broken and fragile, like it rested unsettled upon a fault line that ran down to the core of all I knew to be real—and all I thought I knew about God. I believed God was there somewhere, but mostly because of the knowledge I had acquired from the past. The knowledge of God was all in my head. My heart couldn't sense Him. It was splintered and shattered. And even the pieces of my heart, which felt lifetimes away from each other, were deeply bruised and frayed.

Something—everything—was wrong within me. I appeared normal, but something had unalterably changed in my heart. It was as if my heart lay uncomfortably and unknowingly outside my chest.

I felt disconnected from most moments, not intentionally hiding from the world but totally lost, despite hope that strong belief in God would be an acceptable reason to expect her healing.

---

1   Ernest Hemingway, *A Farewell to Arms* (New York: Scribner, 1995), 193.

Part disbelief, some confusion . . . an event completely unresolved . . . too deep to measure and too far away to touch.

I didn't know if this was normal when people suffered grief and loss. If it was, I couldn't imagine how others found their way through it. Maybe they never did.

I knew people who lost loved ones and then lost themselves in waves of grief and sadness. Loneliness ensued . . . or perhaps, pursued. They remained detached, regardless of what was going on around them. No matter how bright and warm the day, they continually seemed disconnected from happiness. I could see it in their faces. It was as if they couldn't leave the scene of a tragic accident even years after the site was cleared. Whispers of their past lives hung in the air of memories.

My heart was badly broken—unattached to life and the present.

For months, I could still hear the awful silence echoing in the moments after the nurse disconnected the machines and monitors . . . seconds after my wife stopped breathing and died. No whispers of faith . . . no trust . . . just a cold, lonely quiet.

Loss: detriment, disadvantage, or deprivation from failure to keep, have, or get; the state of being deprived of or of being without something that one has had.

We all suffer loss at some point. Sometimes we can see the loss coming. Other times it breaks through the front door of life like a robber, and takes what belongs to you. The trouble with loss is insecurity. It dislodges us from a secure life and leaves us changed, our lives bored out and empty:

the man sitting, face buried in hands, now jobless;
the woman floating in the echoing words of her doctor,
who explains the diagnosis that threatens life today
    and tomorrow;
the parent losing a child to death far too early;
the girl left undone emotionally by the boy
    who promised love.

We all experience loss. Life doesn't always go our way. We grieve as life turns, despite our wanting it not to. In protest, pleading and praying, we fight to maintain the life we know and want. Our faith and our prayers take the shape of our struggle, and hope evaporates in the heat of a life burning out of control. We stand apart from what we knew and loved, a refugee longing for home, a victim lost in pity and unfair circumstance, a doubter and accuser cursing the loss . . . while losing even more.

We become a crumbling wall. Once strong and stable, supported by life going our way, we have little reason not to believe and hope. But when things go badly, the weight of worry, loss, confusion, and grief threaten to break it down.

God is called into question. Is He good . . . really?

Is He not bigger than our pain? Can't He do something about our circumstances?

The paradox of bad things happening to good people surfaces during times of unexplainable tragedy. But what of good things happening to bad people? Is that also not okay? Do we complain about that?

Our concepts of "good" and "bad" question God's sovereignty. In loss, we must see higher than earth. We have to look past the emotion and tragedy to the sky and eternity. We must spy God in the details and believe He is beautifully redeeming even the most damnable pain.

Marianne's death didn't crush me. That was never what I feared most. What posed much more terror was beginning a new life without her. More than being lost or alone or choking in grief, it was the sensation of being detached from the core of all that I believed. The rock on which I supposedly stood was being engulfed by cold and empty waves. Each day was the continuation of the worst dream I could imagine. When I recognized the distance in my daughters' eyes, innocence disturbed, dismay in their hearts where only goodness had prevailed, it terrified me. Three little princesses lost and lonely, wandering through a barren land with their heart-shrunken king of a dad—who felt much more like a court jester without a cheap trick in hand.

Sleeping was good because I usually didn't recall my dreams. It was an escape, the relief of being apart from the struggle. The day was inescapably real. All that I believed could happen, the promise of reality giving way to faith and trust defeating the dreadfulness of tragedy, didn't happen.

Faith failed me, or maybe life was just too much for me. Maybe God's course felt too pre-planned. Maybe my expectations for the future were too bright, so the dark tragedy of death didn't fit the picture I had created. Maybe it didn't really matter. Maybe I didn't even care.

I couldn't focus my thoughts on the new reality and the new challenges. Nothing was normal. Waking up alone was abnormal. It was strange not saying good morning to anyone before the girls woke up.

Being a stranger in my own life was disorienting. I followed similar patterns, held to familiar routines, and interacted with the same people each day. Yet I teetered between falling apart and playing the role of the person I had been.

I spoke about things I knew in my life, but as an observer. I mostly said the right things, but my words had an echo to them.

The sensation of living half a step behind felt completely normal. I wasn't ready to catch up. I knew I could no longer be in the life I loved, but I didn't know how to live in *this* life. No day was normal. In fact, normal wasn't normal. Each day brought a heaviness that weighed on me, pushed me aside, and forced me to the same dead end I couldn't stand revisiting. All the while, I smiled and waited for the next moment, when hopefully the sun would shine a little brighter and life would snap back.

In order to get through each day, I divided time into the shortest possible segments. Wake up. Get the girls ready for school. Drop them off at school. Get ready for work. Start the workday. Make it to lunch. Make it to the end of the workday. Get home and see the girls—the day would get better then. Dinner. Baths. Family time. Bedtime. Repeat.

That was the only way I made it through each day. If I thought too far ahead, worry consumed me, fear dwarfed me, and loneliness drowned me. Sometimes thinking about the evening in the morning or dinner during lunch was too stressful. Reducing time to short increments helped me live through each day.

Smaller segments of time were bearable. I set goals I could meet and gave myself permission to quit if I became overwhelmed. And I did. It was as if I could function in the outside world as long as I kept myself busy, but inside I couldn't escape my constant thoughts. There was no space to hide.

Cognitively, I felt more displaced than angry at God. Yet I couldn't help but feel betrayed, so I would get angry. When that happened, I would tell myself the anger wasn't directed at God, that I was satisfied with the life I had shared with Marianne and that I trusted Him no matter what. That was the conversation in my head and the truth I held to.

My heart was a different story. It was burning with diverse emotions. I often cried on the way to work. I remained lost. Life had made perfect sense to me as part of a couple who knew where we were headed together, what to expect, and how to get there. But now life didn't make any sense at all. The God whom I trusted to lead and take care of me didn't respond as I wanted Him to. Faith faltered. I cried in response to grief, loss, fear, frustration, loneliness, and the goodness that somehow remained present in the midst of the most broken period of my life.

In many ways, my life was completely different. I stumbled and shuffled like someone drunk, acting like I was in control and okay, while it was clear to everyone that I wasn't. I shared this observation frequently with those around me. I repeated myself a lot and had the same conversations with friends. Being connected to grief meant that I couldn't go for long periods of time without reminders. Time was disturbed. Disrupted.

Grief doesn't adhere to a practical or sensible order or time. Life becomes disjointed and askew. Grief is an organic undoing, a loss and enduring absence of someone or something loved . . . an imposed metamorphosis.

"I think you're just depressed, Guy," a friend said rather easily and forthrightly.

Depression made sense. I barely made it through days that seemed to unravel into emptiness. I struggled to find value in most things and in most days. My friend was right. I was depressed and lost in empty, hollow feelings.

A terrible sadness . . . a shrinking of most things good . . . life was too broken and painful to remain the way it was. I tried to get by and make the best out of the worst, to get to the end of each day, but I felt haunted because I couldn't inflate my burst sense of happiness.

Every day I experienced a lingering tiredness: mentally, physically, and spiritually.

Depression was an unwanted guest, but it served a beneficial purpose. It slowed my pace. All I wanted to do was retreat to a safe spot in life and escape as much hurt as possible. Feelings of depression tuned me toward life again as I engaged in grief. Depression gave me the space to process the ugliness of losing so much.

. . . . .

"My name is Guy. My wife died six months ago. I have three daughters. Two of them are with me tonight. My oldest daughter's name is Elizabeth. She's eight years old. My younger daughter is Emily. She's six. My youngest is too young to be here. She's three. Her name is Chloe. She goes to ballet while we come here."

I remember my first GriefWorks meeting. Sitting there quietly, I listened as each person talked about the darkest times in his or her life. Mothers, fathers, husbands, wives, and others spoke of the deep loss of a dear loved one. I was lost in their stories of heartache, separation, and healing. Some used words that hinted at how haunted they were even months and years later. Others seemed to have progressed a safe distance from their pain, dealing with it as they could, and enjoying frequent good days. A few stood out as they spoke with a humble strength that only scars could support.

Then it was my turn. For the first time since my wife's funeral, I spoke about her to people I didn't know. They didn't know me either, but our tears instantly connected us. We were all familiar with the pain of loss. Our pain made us feel different from everyone else in our normal day, but alike as we sat in a circle and confessed to emotions that got the best of us and to questions that lingered.

I was one of the ones trying to maintain a safe distance from my loss, dealing with it as I could, progressing on good days. My hands were clammy as it got closer to my turn to speak. I could feel my face grow flush. I didn't want to be emotional. I just wanted to get through it. I hurried through the part about losing my wife. I gave simple details and focused on the good that was present in my life, the great life we had lived together, the wonderful memories, and my beautiful daughters. I could tell that they were okay that I shared in this way. My feelings and difficulties were nothing new to them.

We met twice a month on Tuesdays and shared a meal served by a local church. We started with small talk and regular details about life that connected us a little more. After the meal we broke into groups arranged according to age, so the kids were together and could process grief at their own pace.

After our first time attending GriefWorks, my girls seemed a little different in the way they spoke, the ease with which they shared, and the way they talked about the future. It was healing for me to see such improvement in their lives. I had been worried that losing their mom at such a young age might derail them, but now I sensed something different: not worry or despair or pain, but hope. They found consolation in meeting kids their age who had experienced loss on the same level. For the first time, they didn't feel weird, alone, or different from everyone else. We all long to be found and to fit in.

Death had stolen life and hope from those people. Others, like me, floated through some of their days. I hoped my conversations helped them, even though they knew I was just as hurt and lost. When they described what they had learned, it was nothing profound. Usually, they shared the name of a new friend, a unique craft, or a funny story. But they were learning how to grieve appropriately, and they were becoming healthier.

A lot happened within me the first year after Marianne's death. In many ways, I became someone else, someone I'm still learning about. For starters, God is someone or something I never quite knew Him to be.

I'm thankful for each improvement, though there are still hard days . . . dark days. But the sun always rises again to warm all that has grown cold in the darkness of night.

CHAPTER EIGHT

9 Degrees

"In the midst of winter, I found there was,
within me, an invincible summer."

—Albert Camus

IT WAS 9 DEGREES outside, and my heart was cold.

No one was around. No voices to be heard, no schedule to attend to, and nothing to do but sit near the fire. I was alone in a cabin where no one knew me and no one cared. I was surrounded by warm light and a comforting silence, yet a complete emptiness swept over me.

Death can be described in many ways. Call it by any name, it's still an ending—a finality no one can defy. We all die—that truth is undeniable—but when death comes, you feel robbed.

My wife died suddenly and unexpectedly.

As a means of dealing with the pain of loss and the sting of death, I had kept busy and insulated, for the most part, from a bottomless heart.

I could feel the emptiness and grief late at night when the kids were in bed and the house was quiet. An uncomfortable silence consumed my security and reduced me to a desperate plea. I wanted what I couldn't have—Marianne no longer existed in this world. I was alone when I didn't want to be.

I buried the pain as deep as possible and did all I could to lose myself so I didn't fall apart or melt down. The path of my life no longer showed two sets of footprints, our footprints together, but I had a great responsibility to three little lives. They were watching me, searching for stability. I felt like a small kid standing on a high diving board, petrified by fear—frozen by the distance between the board and the surface of the water. But just as the cheers of his friends convince him to take the courageous plunge, I lived through each day fueled by a determination to be there for my daughters.

I prayed to be kept a healthy distance from the terrible darkness in my heart and dreams. I begged God to protect my daughters' hearts, to guide them through each day, and to allow them not to be scarred. I pleaded for their lives to stabilize and for me to find strength to guide and nourish them.

Meanwhile, the surface of my heart grew thinner, and the darkness pushed up with violent force. Each day I grew more numb, playing a role, clinging fiercely to a misappropriated responsibility.

I was living for my daughters. They were all that remained identifiable and real from the life that was no more. Living for my daughters—for their happiness, for their future, for their security—seemed more than honorable and heroic. It was all there was to live for, all that mattered.

So I kept sinking.

A trusted friend saw me slipping below the surface. He said to expect the sinking grief and to make room for it. He assured me that God was big enough to find me in every moment, no matter how low I descended.

I needed such steady reassurance, but of course, it didn't right all that had gone wrong. Most days I didn't know what made sense anymore.

As time passed and reality settled into my psyche, I realized I could no longer deal with life at a distance. My heart was bleeding out, bursting in unplanned, awkward moments. Deep down, something hadn't been addressed, resolved, or healed. I had been ignoring, neglecting, and distancing myself from it. My loss was like a silhouette or a shadow, following me and always present.

I felt pain and loneliness, hurt and anger.

In an effort to survive, to string together any sense in my grief, I made plans to get away by myself for a few days. I couldn't take another step pretending to be the brave hero of my situation, all the while shrinking inside. I wanted to escape to the mountains without my phone, without my computer, and without distractions. I needed to strip as much as I could out of my days so I could let all the pain bleed out.

Somehow the air in the mountains felt stiffer than the buried memories fighting to surface. It felt like lonely space awaiting my arrival. The grief I had kept at a distance couldn't be ignored in the quiet. It loomed large to find me as I hid in that mountain cabin. It was time to deal with my shattered heart.

I had come to the cabin to breathe, to release the tension of loss that had accumulated with each day of my new life. But sitting alone in the cabin, I felt a million miles away from anything helpful and hopeful. God didn't feel big. *Life* felt big . . . and overwhelming. It wasn't supposed to be this way.

More than loneliness, anger stirred in me. I had lost my wife—the reality of this seemed to bind itself to every thought that passed through my mind. I just wanted to forget the sound of her voice, the feel of her touch, the thoughts we had shared, the promises we had made.

During the day I hiked, mountain-biked through shallow creeks, and explored the terrain. In the expanse of daylight, with no gadgets or to-do lists crowding in, I had room to distance myself from the swirling emotions. At times, I thought clearly and prayed to a hearing God.

But night . . .

Night felt completely different. It felt constricted, too close. With no activities to distract my mind, I sat alone inside the small cabin by a crackling fire. In this narrower space, my thoughts were heavy and preoccupied.

I vented. I prayed. I wondered.

Lost in quick-firing thoughts, I tried to piece together why life had turned out this way and how in the world I had ended up where I was.

I never imagined life taking so much from me so quickly.

All of my musings seemed a variation of a single thought that drew blood from my already wounded, raging heart.

How could You let this happen?

We only tried to give You our lives.

Above all, we mostly tried to live our lives for You.
And we were happy to do it.
When I needed You most, when I asked for You to save her,
You didn't.
I still don't get it.
I'm so lost.

Silence . . . a fire burning inside . . . a cold wind howling outside.

I don't remember if those were only thoughts in my mind or if I spoke the words aloud. Either way, they screamed from my heart, escaping into the silent sky where God was too far to feel or find. And when they did, my anxious thoughts stopped and time slowed to a halt.

Throughout the first day at the cabin, my thoughts were fast and anxious. I guarded myself with noble activity, trying not to stop long enough to let tragedy seep in . . . trying not to embrace the horrible truths boiling inside of me. After all, this trip had a purpose. Like a holy hero on a noble quest for deeper meaning, I had journeyed into the mountains to get better. I was attempting to self-medicate my soul. The only problem was, it wasn't working. I was there to find something. What I would discover is that Something needed to find me.

For the first time, I realized how deeply I was wounded. Since my wife's death, I hadn't been still long enough to see it. I had kept busy with heavy responsibilities, faith, and other fruitless activity—hiding in my schedule. My mind kept tidy with compartmentalized effort.

I remembered my mother-in-law's voice when she told me the paramedics were rushing to the hospital with my wife. I relived standing and watching ER nurses and doctors rush around her body as she coded. I recalled sitting beside her as she lay in bed, machines breathing for her.

I decided it was enough.

I had heard the beeping stop and her breaths cease. Then I had closed her eyes and said goodbye one last time.

I had pulled it together enough to find words for my daughters. I had picked out her casket and watched it lowered into the earth. I had held my daughters, collapsing. I had breathed in deeply and tried to keep going. All the while, questions hung unsettled and unanswered.

I had held it together until that bitter cold night, alone beside the fire. I sat suspended in heavy moments and beautifully haunting memories for what felt like a long time. Minutes? Hours? And then . . . I broke.

Tears streamed as I asked, "How could You? Why would You?" Somehow I knew that no answer would be satisfactory. I realized my questions weren't about loss, loneliness, or grief as much as they were about presence . . . trust . . . God.

"If You weren't there when I needed You most, when will You be? Where will You be?" Tears streamed freely.

Like a criminal seeing the light of day suddenly unframed by cinderblocks, I sensed a route to freedom through my tears. I missed Marianne incomprehensibly, but I knew fully well she had died. It was unchangeable—life would never be the same again. In the days now and ahead, could I trust? What about the next tragedy?

A daunting task lay in front of me, and I didn't want to face it. I had to say goodbye. I had to let go of that life. I needed to, but I didn't know how. The smell of timber, the stones around the chimney and walls, the cold air, the quiet—it all felt lonely, like a prison where no thoughts could escape into a busy schedule of responsibilities and activity.

My heart couldn't do it. It couldn't maintain distance. It could no longer hold together without breaking, without collapsing. Each day felt like a held breath with no exhale. I needed relief.

Like the tide relentlessly pushing warm waves onto the shore, Jesus, the Man of Sorrows acquainted with grief, washed over wounds still open and raw. Then and there, with earth holding and sky redeeming, both collided as grace overpowered grief and love surrounded loss.

I exhaled honestly in the silence of two worlds colliding, with one kingdom winning and a Savior finding. For the first time, I didn't seek answers or an explanation for why my wife had died or why my young daughters had lost their mommy. The eyes of my heart were directed toward a dawning tomorrow.

Hope.

Love reminded me why the loss hurt so much. I had memories that death could never touch, destroy, or take away. Our days together would live forever. They were our days, and we had lived them together as deeply as we could . . . loving, not fearing an end.

I always wondered about the sanity of people who claimed to be visited by angels or by Jesus, and of the validity of their experiences.

Nothing extraordinary happened in that cabin. I didn't see or hear choirs of angels. But Jesus came. And He sat still as I spoke words hidden under the wreckage of my heart. I released thoughts I had pushed aside. I poured out pieces I had been trying to put back together, pieces that didn't fit anymore.

I didn't see Him or hear Him. I didn't touch Him or feel Him. But strangely enough, I didn't need to. He was undeniably present, fully understanding, and deeply healing.

I learned a lot about trust and God's love that night. Time passed as cold winds howled outside the cabin, while sheltered inside, lost in warmth, my heart bled everything toxic. There in the quietness of the night, a new strength filled me. Life felt more vibrant and colorful with each new thought.

I had much to live for.

The pressure to be bigger than the pain and loss, to be the hero I thought my daughters needed, dissipated. The redirection was subtle, but it was enough of a correction to give room for new life. Now my focus would be to live like life still mattered—because it did. It was a paradox: When I lived exclusively and fully for my daughters, they got less of me, but when I walked the path to become whole and strong, they got more of me. I was determined to live with the passion and focus they had seen when Marianne and I lived together, and they would draw strength from it.

And again, I knew I wasn't really alone.

When I look back I see God's great faithfulness. He has carefully guided me, directing me to this day. And here I am, having been led through the darkest of days and loneliest of nights, the most treacherous path I ever have walked. And my heart is alive despite the scandalous thieving of the one I loved.

What shapes my faith in God? Will He suddenly lose care, concern, or ability? Has He finally met His match? I should think not and always hope not. He doesn't lose heart. We do.

I do . . . still, and often.

Even in the wake of inconceivable grace, my heart still wilts sometimes. Circumstance is captivating. It can divert my attention with ease.

Where is God? The question resurfaces.

And I'm left again with the same questions—and even bigger ones. Can God help a person in his most difficult time? Will He help . . . a life coming undone?

If He can't help you during the unexplainable, unexpected, and unfortunate times, can you consider Him any help at all?

When your job folds and money dries up . . .

When your family's security is threatened by mounting bills . . .

When your marriage is tested or comes apart . . .

When your teenager runs away . . .

When a friend or family member ruins life with an addiction . . .

Can God help in the "what-if's" of life?

What if my daughters stray from the path I've shown them? What if they push away the nurturing love I offer?

Is God who He says He is? Is He enough?

After news of an incurable diagnosis . . .

When death surprises you and does not leave . . .

Is He still, inside of all this and apart from all of this, *God?*

. . . . .

I am dangerously holding,

disappearing beneath wave's surface foaming,

tossing and beating,

losing and dreaming,

eyes that uncover the hand folding,

the lights bright blinking.

I am afraid of the door closing,

fading in the sound creaking,

bending and bowing,

seeping and hoping,

my hand warm on the knob turning

yesterday, leaving.

In wonderful and seemingly endless moments, life gives so fully. No worry is too big or too consuming. We move along. All is well and undisturbed. We count life as good. Our hearts give thanks for all we have. A warm home, secure and safe with a full cupboard. Kids running in bare feet in the cool grass, laughter filling the air. Contentment that generates honest smiles. This is what we work hard for and aim to have, all that we need and want. This is good.

But as much as we hope life will always be this way, it won't. Circumstance is part consequence, part predicament, and all mystery. It is cause and effect, and we can't always connect the dots.

Our decisions and choices lead us down the path. At all times and in every situation, no matter how quickly they appear or how heavy they are, we hold the power to choose.

Back in the cabin with the wind wailing in the cold night, that's what prompted my breakthrough: the uncontrollable, the unexplainable, the moments in life demanding why. Marianne's death . . . three little girls left without their mother . . . no explanation on this side of life. It is what it is. Life breaks and we're frail, much more than we imagined when we enjoyed an undisturbed, peaceful sky.

Now I can identify this loss as the greatest opportunity of my life. It's strange, but true. That insight brings me great joy now, but it was quite a journey getting to that point. I had to resettle my faith and my ideas about God.

While we can't always control circumstance, we *can* master our response to Christ's precise awareness and unending care for us. We are human beings, disciples who proclaim themselves helpless, needing rescue by a Savior. In storms at night, howling winds push through darkness in different directions. A captain hears the sound of waves smashing into the bow and stern and sides of the boat— it's disorienting.

The disciples, some of them seamen, were familiar with boat and sea, and yet in stormy waters they were as frightened as novices. They were faithful followers of Jesus, but in the face of crashing waves as faithless as those who didn't know Him. They experienced a circumstance they couldn't control: the boat creaking and groaning, their friends fearful and yelling, and Jesus sleeping through it all until someone shakes Him awake.

Jesus rebuked the wind and the waves. He changed circumstances.

The question the disciples asked breaks to the surface of our lives as well. Where is He? When we need Him, where will He be? Does He know fully well?

This is the ageless question asked by everyone drowning in painful, uncontrollable circumstance. Where is He? He's present in dark times, when powerful waves grind against the sides of our faith, when we're disoriented by suddenly changing conditions. No matter the severity or the suffering, Christ remains aware.

When our distress flags wave and we can withstand no more, when we float lost in the frailty of all that we are and have become, we can still be assured that God is good. His power isn't diminished by changing conditions. His goodness lies in His unmatchable ability to redeem and make uncontrollable wrongs right.

Jesus asked His disciples, "Why are you afraid? Have you still no faith?"

Their feet were soaked. Their hearts still pounded. They still drew breaths deep and out of rhythm. . . . but everything was eerily calm. The threatening wind suddenly was no more. The water was as still and flat as glass. Jesus was wet, too, yet His eyes were calm, as if nothing had happened. He understood why His friends had been terrified. He had seen the waves; He had heard the howling wind. But He wanted them to see something else. Now. Afterward certainly, but even now.

"Why are you afraid?" invites us out of the wind and waves, beyond our panic and dread, and into His moment of security. Afterward. Even then.

We're just like them—transfixed by the storm, wondering when it will stop (or kill us), waiting for people and love to make sense again. We expected a life so bright, right there at our doorstep. In our sorrow, we try to make it right, but we only make it worse. Finally, we find the One who can still the storm in our souls. That's grief. Embracing yesterday and wishing it well. Embracing now and holding it tight. Wanting so badly to be whole now.

So what, then? Faith. Have you none?

I realized my life would be ruined if I didn't let go of fear. I had to endure the storm of what-ifs and hope-nots. Fear consumes us when we can't let go. We run around in panic and assume the painful present will last forever. Life ebbs and flows, circumstances threaten to swamp our lives, but hope exists even in quiet thoughts. After the darkest of nights, the morning will bring a new dawn. Fear had consumed me and changed me, altering words and perspective. The problem, I realized, was the fear of losing, not the losing itself. Loss is the lasting reality left in the wake of fear.

Grief isn't just sorrow. It includes faith in the future. It's releasing what can no longer be and becoming open to new possibilities. I have to trust that Jesus is standing there right in front of me. He is wet, too. He never left me during the stormy moments. His eyes are calm, loving, and patient. He sees my panic, calms the storm, and whispers, "Why are you afraid?"

CHAPTER NINE

Surely Goodness and Mercy

I SAW A MAN ALONE, subdued by pain, frightened by all that might someday be. A man stumbling, drunk on why things turned out the way they did, mumbling angrily to himself—a man clinging to fading memories like a thief clutching a leaking bag.

I quietly asked not to become that man. I couldn't. I wouldn't be him. I refused to be afraid of shadows and terrified of the future. My daughters will never know that man. They might see me wince and wrestle with life's haunting questions, but they will never know that man who has a hollowed heart and is comfortable only in isolation. I may not have much more to offer than my courage, but my healing will be an echo that resounds like bells of freedom in their hearts.

And their little hearts will be warm. I couldn't leave us stranded on the roadside and stuck forever in hurt, loss, and sorrow. I couldn't let pain unravel the strongest of loves, ours, sewn together by life's untroubled waters and God's goodness.

Life may indeed seem to take days, memories, and happiness from us, but courage is mine. At its source, it's immeasurably and unfathomably deep. It's unending. Through darkened spots and failing strength, courage remains.

Life was good, but goodness was suspended with Marianne's death, lessening those of us who remained, those who loved her most.

But the days continued. And they demanded to be lived.

We were still a family, less one. We still had our life together, as well as love, now, and tomorrow. Smiles eventually began to appear on our faces again despite occasional fierce pangs of grief and lonely nights when memories of the one taken away from us dwarfed even the most powerful resolve we had felt during the day.

I sensed the continuing of life during conversations with my daughters. While they missed their mother grievously, their hearts reached for more. They began to pull life out of my stalled heart as they questioned tomorrow.

What will our lives look like?

Where will we live? What will we do?

Who will do our hair?

Who will get us ready for school?

Who will take us shopping?

I remember Elizabeth asking, "Dad, what about my sweet sixteen?"

Before the healing began, I had no room for such questions in my day-to-day thinking. The hurt was spoiling inside my heart, haunting every new day. I had lived with the hurt of losing my wife, of God not answering my prayers for her healing, and especially of my young daughters crying themselves to sleep as I sat with no answers. But there was something beyond resilience in my little girls' hearts that was absent in mine: their ability to find goodness in today and hope in tomorrow—and accept it independent of everything else.

It was as if their little hearts called out to mine while it was fumbling and frozen, "What now, dad? Where will we go? What will we do? Will you take us?"

That was precisely how I began to find my way again. In my daughters I saw tomorrow, and I felt the desire again for life. I also saw myself in them—a frightened child wounded, wondering, hoping that God could and would piece life back together again . . . somehow.

Strength emerged from the fog of grief that had shrouded my heart from most things bright and hopeful. I grew determined to go at life headlong and figure out the details as we went into the new day. This became a regular theme in all areas of our family. Rather than remaining stuck and sinking, we learned to accept the reality that brought death into our family and to embrace life so we could move forward. We moved steadily away from that darkest moment into the potential of each new day.

We were in terra incognita, a world unknown. Never before had I been a single parent, and I didn't have a strategy to shift to a solo role. Add to that the weight of loss and grief, and I knew we would be traveling uphill most of the way. Yet piecing life back together for them and for me provided a welcome challenge—a new adventure.

So I set out to lead us. We were leaving behind a place in life that we had loved, and we were seeking a new place to grow together, to live fully again.

I had wrestled with questions in the quiet, doubted God's protection and involvement, lost myself in what-if scenarios, and felt defeated at the enormity of trying to pull life together. Yet all of my activity had not provided the answers I craved until I dissociated from the lofty and engaged in the simple with my daughters. It is always in the simple things that I find God in the fullest ways.

Life in small, simple steps. It was a path our feet could travel, not too treacherous or overgrown with complexities, but easy and in the moment. We had to find a different pace and learn anew how to relate to one another, how to depend on one another, and how to live life together.

We had always known togetherness. Now my girls realized they had only a dad to lead, support, nurture, and shape them. I was a single dad with three little ladies nipping at my heels as I wandered through the day looking for stability.

Worry gripped my heart.

How would my three daughters grow into young women? How could I be the father they needed me to be?

In nearly every way, I felt unprepared for life alone with them. I had an amazing relationship with each of my daughters, but it had always been in the context of our family prior to Marianne's death. Being a dad had come natural and easy, but now, our family dynamic had radically changed. Without the balance of both parents, they got the best of me and the worst of me.

After several months stalled in grief and barely making it through most days, it became apparent that we wouldn't make it much longer unless something changed. And so, we did. We realized we had to create new patterns, new habits, and new traditions. Only then would we make real progress. Slowly, with a new thankfulness for each day lived well, we began the transition from one life to another. The scars were not yet closed, but our hearts were hungry and hopeful.

One new tradition had to happen in the kitchen. I didn't know how to cook, but fast food and restaurants had created the feeling of a transitional, temporary family when we craved permanence and stability. We needed to use our kitchen, so we agreed to cook as a family. We started small—once a week—and we made it fun.

I concluded that homemade pizza counted as a meal and couldn't possibly be too difficult to make. While the pizza wasn't quite as easy as I anticipated, it boasted a variety of toppings when we finally slid it into the stove. We waited a few minutes, took our creation out of the oven, sliced it, and had our first meal together. It was a small but significant victory. A sense of accomplishment filled our hearts. The kitchen looked lived in for the first time in months.

My mother moved in with us to help. She cooked some nights throughout the week, but one evening each week was entirely ours. The countertops were piled high with messes from our efforts and ingredients. I took pictures to commemorate the events. I felt like an enthusiastic parent dropping a kid off at kindergarten for the first time. As I look back at those photographs, I can see the transformation. We found hope in the simple, in the resumption of normal life. In our new normal, we found goodness again. I found God again right there in the simple, almost uneventful undertaking of living each day again.

Day by day we found more simple things to do. Slowly, new traditions formed. I started each morning with a simple prayer: "Father, thank You for all this day holds."

"Surely goodness and mercy shall follow me all the days of my life." The ancient psalmist-king's words began to echo loudly in my heart. Loss had threatened to reduce me to a victim of sadness in which the absence of my wife and the life we knew redefined my life forever. For a while, goodness had no space.

How could life be good in the wake of life gone so wrong? The words from Psalm 23 that I once mindlessly memorized as a child surfaced with new glory, reaching for me even as I descended in despair. But then, hope. Light. Newness. All invading the darkness to restore a life maligned and misshapen by death.

The idea of goodness "following me" counteracted my fear about moving forward. I was able to move into tomorrow . . . into hope, into rediscovering joy, and into full, meaningful life . . . by experiencing every new day as a sacred gift from God. The distance between earth and sky was measured in holy prayers and simple steps—in hands that made pizza together and released one day gone for another arriving.

By no means did we marginalize grief, ignore the crushing emotion and stark depression, or move forward in desperation to escape the haze of grief covering each day. We hurt honestly and openly with friends and family, and even more in the strong-yet-frail company of one another. We grew brave in the dark, and resolute in God's stated version of how our story would continue. Surely goodness and mercy (steadfast, loyal love) will follow us all the days of our lives.

To perceive God as good (or bad) based on circumstantial evidence is to judge Him on events I deem acceptable and appropriate. It's a flawed perspective that shifts according to circumstances. My view of His goodness fluctuates with how I feel—how I understand

and interpret the circumstances unfolding around me. It becomes a cavernous problem and inevitably leads to heartache.

The goodness of God is far bigger, higher, and more mysterious than we can ever imagine. My definitions and understanding have nothing to do with His goodness and mercy. Even if I can't grasp His goodness, He is still good, kind, loving, just, and merciful—because that is His essential nature. All good in our lives finds its source in God and reverberates throughout creation. We can trust in God's goodness even in our pain, tragedy, and brokenness. Even in our most tentative steps forward, God relentlessly leads, guides, pursues, follows, and surrounds.

· · · · ·

To inglorious depth You have pursued,
to own glory where evil trod
and laid flat seas tossing unholy.

With a new resolve and hope, I set a deliberate pace forward, while allowing room for grief to create a lasting strength for my girls and myself. I couldn't change or ignore what had happened. Marianne's death was tragic. We couldn't go back and start over again. We couldn't relive those wonderful days before she collapsed. We either had to go forward or exist in shadows . . . and as shadows.

In going forward, we found that goodness followed.

Grief can be polarizing: you feel isolated and alone. You no longer belong to what was, and you don't yet belong to what will be. It isn't a fleeting feeling or controllable emotion. Emotions swell and recede in memories. Grief exists in the void of something loved no longer existing.

In my grief and the transition between one life over and the new beginning, I grew into someone different. In the months after Marianne's death, while patching life in stitched-together fashion through the simple act of preserving some traditions and forging new ones, our family grew stronger and began to resurface with a new identity. We even developed a sense of adventure. In addition to learning to cook together, we got to know each other more deeply than ever before. We had wonderful conversations about life and emotions of sadness, loneliness, and depression. I invested words and activity in a hopeful future.

Perhaps in a stroke of God's divine foresight, we had created a new family routine just a few weeks before Marianne died. It was her idea. She wanted to instill the value of gratitude and grace in our girls' lives. Late one evening, she discussed her idea with me. She suggested we take time to sit quietly together as a family, and one at a time say something that we liked or were thankful for about every other family member that day. I was sold. We called the tradition "circle time." After Marianne died, the girls and I continued to engage each other in circle time most nights before bed.

We also established a new tradition (for us, anyway) of daddy-daughter dates. Excitement filled their hearts on their date day. As for me, entering into their worlds in conversation and experiences was like stumbling upon unexpected treasure or cresting a hilltop to see a breathtaking summer sunrise. Our dates have been treasured times—for me and for them. Their words would express fears and deep sadness in one breath, and then speak of the goodness of life in the next. My girls awakened me to hope and joy. Far more than they may ever know, they propped me up and called the man out of me.

When I became a single parent, I no longer had a choice about how much effort to give. The girls looked to me for everything.

"Dad, what should I wear?"

"What should I get my friend for her birthday?"

"Can you do my hair?"

"Can we go and get a manicure?"

"Dad, I think I need a bra."

"Dad, what is sex?"

The first few months as a single dad felt like an absolute whirlwind. I was widowed, and they were motherless and grieving. Emotions ran deep and erupted frantically at times. Many of those early days were spent searching for any space where we could feel comfortable in our family. Granted, I had enormous support from my mother, who has been nothing short of amazing, but at the end of the day, I am my daughters' only parent. It is both my privilege and responsibility to show them the way and lead them into tomorrow.

I say to them often, especially in difficult times when they are hurting or frustrated, "God gave you me and me you, and He didn't make a mistake."

Honestly, though, sometimes I was as lost in parenting as I was in grief. I wasn't just a dad. I was, and would be from that time forward, a parent—open to life with my three beautiful daughters through the pain, the hurting, the confusion, and the loneliness.

I went for a walk under a starlit sky, finding hope and returning as a different man. The stars made sense in a whole new way. They hung perfectly, millions of miles away, positioned precisely and shining brightly, as if broadcasting a message of hope throughout the endless panoramic expanse of the night sky. They represented order, security, and future. They raptured me away from living as a victim. I felt closer to God that night standing under the stars, His stars, and asking Him to help me build the family that we, my wife and I, once started together.

Slowly over the next few weeks, we began to grow again. I wasn't as worried about how to raise three little girls. I would raise them in our new context and our new reality.

I introduced them to adventure to keep their hearts curious and growing. We attacked our weaknesses together. I learned how to tie a ponytail, and they learned how to fish. They taught me how to paint nails, and I showed them how to scout a hiking trail. Our life together will always be a beautiful treasure.

I had worried that parenting three little girls would be the most difficult challenge in my new life as a single parent. But as God's goodness blossomed into life, that role became the gravitational centerpiece to our healing. Everything became an adventure.

One day my daughters will think of the man they saw, the dad they knew, the words I spoke, our time together . . . and those thoughts of me will guide them. I'm sure they will also recall my shortcomings, inadequacies, mistakes, failures, and times when I was selfish, insensitive, angry, and frustrated. The list of my flaws can go on and on. Trust me. But I believe they can learn valuable lessons from those times, as well. And that will be a good thing.

My responsibility to them is simple: love them and lead them. I can show them how to love by loving them. I can show them how to live by undergoing life's circumstances with them. I can teach them the value of grace and the reality of God by living each day reflecting God's beautiful, unexplainable love.

One day, not so far in the future, they will no longer bear my name, but my desire is that their hearts will always resemble my heart. I want them to know from me how to identify the next heart that they unswervingly commit to. From the moment they choose another man, I want them to walk confidently with each step, to know who they are and how to live and love. One of my greatest accomplishments as their daddy will be preparing them to choose wisely.

At some point, hopefully in the far and distant future, I will only be a memory to them. On that day, I want them to look back—as far as they can remember—and be warmed by good memories of our life well lived.

If I do my job, the memory of me will warm and comfort them. I hope they never forget their mother's death and my feeble heart strengthened by God's love, the house where we created a home, our traditions and habits, and finally, how God redeemed our situation and led us into a bright new day. That's where we are right now. It's a fresh day where hope is strong, love is present, and tomorrow is a shining reality.

I want God to be present and welcome in each of their mundane routines and in every dire circumstance. I want them to trust God's hand and heart in everything, and never think of Him as an add-on or a secondary priority. It is not enough to try to squeeze God into our schedule at bedtime or as a corrective reference point. I want to live, and I want my girls to live, with the reality that God is supremely present in everything. As they grow and my role changes—and later even, when I am no longer around—God will be the same to them. Everything. In every day, both now and in all their tomorrows, goodness will exist as surely as the sun will rise and their lungs will fill. Perhaps the greatest loss in grief is the erasure of hope. In the crushing pain, life feels too large to deal with, too broken to mend. All hope dissipates in the dark, cold days. Memories haunt lonely nights that seem to last forever, but goodness always exists because mercy and the fiercest of loves, surely God's love, dwells in all we know and feel.

In the midst of great tragedy, stark depression, and in the simplicity of living life again, goodness and mercy followed me and pushed me onward.

God's Grace, a Hunting Love

our heavenly Father,

Almighty and everlasting God,

who hast safely brought us to the beginning of this day . . .

(The Third Collect for Grace, Book of Common Prayer)

MY EFFORT WAS NOT WHAT SAVED ME.
Neither did my daughters. We couldn't save each other. We
had no sustaining or substantial answers within us. Days, weeks,
and months passed as we sank silently, dealing with grief and
coping, but the shaking wasn't finished. Pieces of who we were
kept crumbling and falling like shards of rock off a mountain. On
my best days, I was insecure, deteriorating in dry winds, looking to
the sky for reprieve . . . for answers. Waiting.

GOD'S GRACE, A HUNTING LOVE   143

My feet stood squarely on the edge. My toes curled around the ledge. I was barely hanging on. Everything before me was shifting, undefined, and dangerous. For years I had lived unhindered, happy, and convinced the path would always be right in front of me. Then a divide cut the path with unspeakable tragedy. It was a deep blow, straight into the gut of my faith.

I knew we couldn't go backward, even though behind us were the most beautiful memories. We stood at the irreconcilable edge of what we knew to be true, and what didn't make sense.

My daughters' little hearts were once innocent and shielded from the cold winds. Now, their stuttering, saddened words hung in tension. I wanted to pick them up and run back to earlier days when their smiles were like sunlit moments . . . warm.

At the same time, I wanted to hold them tighter so they wouldn't lean too far and fall into whatever was ahead. But as I held them in grief and loss, between then and now, memory and moment, my heart faded to a dim flicker. What was right, all that I was told to count on, dissipated as holy echoes at the foot of death.

Death is a certainty for all of us. As sure as life lives and the next day begins, death awaits us at some point. For many, death is perceived as a distant reality, an event that will happen when life slows and many days lay behind. When it arrives unannounced and premature, it is evil, an unapologetic thief.

That's the reason my heart stopped as Marianne's contracted in one last faint beat.

Standing beside her body, which only moments earlier had housed beauty and dreams, I floated away, drifting into a fog. I could sense God in the peace that hummed quietly in the chaos of planning a funeral, shaking hands and smiling, gently assuring everyone of my well-being. I was okay . . . in moments. Broken in others. Already, her death seemed like an impassible divide, a slice of time fractured by tragedy, leaving me unsure of how to resolve it all. When? How?

What if the way we think about God is wrong, tangled and twisted in our view of a cause-and-effect world?

What if God isn't sitting unaffected on the other side?

What if God is closer than we can imagine and more present than we are aware?

What if God is right in the mess of where you think it must end for you, when your heart seizes with fear and night is longer than day?

What if reprieve glimmered real in your darkest night?

When the pain of life threatens to separate us from God, I would imagine most, like me, try to bridge that gap. We want to make sense of it, whether by judging God or justifying what He allows. But life doesn't always make sense, nor does it happen according to plan. Easy answers don't exist for every difficulty. But a solution does.

Grace.

God's grace . . . a hunting love.

It stands, a lighthouse shining in the dark, firm against absorbing and unrelenting waves, providing hope for lost souls. Grace is a calling to a safe harbor in the storm. Grace is an end to the beginning, a restart forevermore.

In our relationships with God, humans are often painted as the pursuers. We search for meaning, strive for improvement, and look for God. We see Him in goodness, in fairness, and in all things right and orderly. He makes sense there. When life is favorable, His existence and presence fit with our beliefs. We believe the words *blessed* and *righteous* to be a pattern for living.

Sometimes, though, life and God don't make sense. Even in Scripture, some words aren't pleasant or comforting: *murder, genocide, war, slavery, betrayal.* Someone loves God enough to fight with everything he has, only to lay with another's wife—then with a heavy heart and humble words he rises again to rule. People falter and flail, bruise and batter, with cowardly hearts and unruly tongues. Are we really the pursuers?

In the beginning, nothing. Quiet. Dark. Lifeless. Not you. Not me. No one. Just One, forever and always, fully alive as only He can be. Not one thing apart from Him sustains . . . or even exists. No record of time or wrong or right.

And into the undefined . . . creation, creation, creation! Light . . . and beauty . . . life invades and unfolds.

We still see details of God everywhere, a trail leading back to His creating hand and His loving heart pursuing human drips of life bearing His own image. He has always been the pursuer.

We think of ourselves as conquerors, looking to possess and rule the world. We plant flags in the ground to claim discovery, ownership, and independence. It's the lie from the garden . . . Eden disturbed. Man's unholy, defiled attempt to gain power resulted instead in a broken world, a lost soul.

And so, the hunt. Through time passing and men failing, Love hunts to recover all that was lost, both then and now. Whispering winds and burning bushes. Creation calling back, "Save us!"

A scandalous love it was, God sending Jesus as a gruesome sacrifice, but man's eyes were closed and his arms folded. God didn't stop. He still searches. He is looking for those still hiding, to expose the lie that man is able to save himself. The Creator made humble in disguise of skin, bone, and blood. Both God and man . . . to ransom man. God: yesterday, today, and forever.

Death reminds us that our hands are never as much in control as we thought. We acknowledge truth at the end, our words confessing that we are small and needy. We all return from where we came. Dust and life are only borrowed.

In all rightness, happiness swings softly in the warm sun cooled by white clouds. Underneath, kids run and play in grass freshly cut . . . making up games without rules . . . living in unkept time. The peace of life unfolds with holiness. Memories are captured in pictures stored away for times when happiness will need to be found again. We remember fondly as we look back at earlier moments.

Sometimes the sun doesn't shine. Life breaks and runs out all messy, ignoring sacredly marked lines and boundaries.

There is no denying the pain. We sit uncomfortable, asking questions that have no answers, groaning for a glimpse of happiness instead of unresolved silence. We sit silently at night, sinking, wishing for words. But words aren't there when a heart is hiding, mute to the world around it.

Smile. Nod. Smile. Silence.

Marianne's death was wrong. It was wrong to snatch away all reason for smiles and simple thanks. My eyes dimmed watching her slowly move out of this existence to one unknown to me, to a place I'm told to trust in, a place shaping life even now. People have died in the name of this place. Others come to life because of its open doors. That's where she rests or runs, where she resides. Not here. Not now. Never again.

I wasn't ready. There were no goodbyes . . . just a life behind us holding happiness. And a small, easily missed flicker in the eyes of my daughters, strong enough to pull me right again. Love lost always finding me. Somehow it was enough.

Months dragged by. I woke to the same day every day, lost and looking for something. Through wreckage, carnage, broken memories, and maimed existence, I fell into each day, both comforted and undone by one certain fact: God was somewhere and somehow involved in the darkness where earth and sky collided.

Grief thins our hearts. Faith and resolve flatten in times too difficult to accept the circumstance as right and okay. Even those who walked and talked with Jesus felt this way.

Jesus' friends ran from the danger of His arrest. Their previous courage dissolved in their fear of suffering the same end as their leader/friend.

Two travelers on the road to Emmaus felt defeated, sinking in hopeless reality. They lost faith because their eyes couldn't see, and their path was covered with complications and questions. Victory had been theirs, but it vanished on the cross . . . or so they thought. Their undeniable encounter with Resurrection hushed their fears and set their hearts burning.

God was writing a new story in the eternal sand of time, changing the world forever with the sacrifice of the cross. He is the Author and Perfecter, not of fables and myths or lullabies sung to comfort a breaking heart, but of true and powerful grace. Life. Reaching hand. Searching Light. Finder. Rescuer. Savior.

Come find me. I cannot see.

• • • • •

Snow fell as I watched from the warmth of our house that used to be a home. As I watched each snowflake drift gently to the ground, all I could think about was the year before when near record levels of snow blanketed the almost always warm Texas ground. The kids ran out in the early morning to greet the snowfall, barely dressed but fully exhilarated. Marianne and I followed. We had a blast. Everyone tracked snow into the house and threw wet clothes onto the wooden floor, but it didn't matter. It was snowing in Texas—recorded in feet that winter, not inches. We played and laughed. Our hearts were free and untainted.

Now, a year later, I was lost in the drift. My heart wasn't free, but bound in tragedy. The girls were with me, but Marianne was not. At night, they would wake up crying. I wanted to tell them their dreams weren't real, but it wasn't true. She was no longer here. The life they knew and loved was no more. It killed me to hear them weep. Hearts, breaking from recent memories, devastated me every time.

That's what I thought of as I watched the snowfall before they woke up. They would remember, as I did, Marianne's smile, her excitement, and how had she held them in the cold of winter. Her lap somehow had room enough for all three. Their words found safety in her heart, an endless spring of love. That heart had a rhythm that paced theirs, always with a deep belonging. She was the one who bore them and nurtured them and knew them. She was a haven and a world of comfort. That's where they knew themselves, in their mother. And that's where I knew them best. On this particular snowy day, they would wake to burning breakfast and ill-advised clothes to wear in the cold. We do it all together—the mistakes and the learning, and we call it our adventure, our new life: a dad raising three little daughters who are dealing with death, life, and all the mess in between. Three little princesses are teaching him how to be whole again.

When life unexpectedly bends and crushes and collapses, we forget who we are and how we got here. Grace guides, lifts, and finds. We are pursued by a hunting love, belonging to Him who created and sustains all creation. Difficulties force us to know Him at a different level. A deeper level . . . wthout the fluff, but stronger, richer, and more real.

My life as I knew it ended when my wife died. One day it existed as it had the day before, a flourishing garden of beautiful blooms. At the end of that day, the garden was crushed, trampled, and ruined. I found the truth and impenetrable theology in the simple explanation I gave to my daughters: "God didn't take mommy from you. He wouldn't do that. God rescued mommy from the pain that her sickness was causing her. Instead of her hurting and being in pain, God brought her to heaven so that she wouldn't hurt or be sick anymore."

And that beauty—that uncovered, treasured reality that God did indeed exist—gave me hope as I shuffled half-heartedly through a lonely valley shadowed by death. When hope evaded the days and memories filled the nights, God weaved Himself into the hurt to comfort me. My feet slipped, my knees buckled, but still I found myself a bit farther down the path each day. In the darkest of times, God remains exactly the same: loving . . . hunting for those who are lost, broken, and hopeless; and rescuing all who will be found. He's not apart, but within and around and throughout.

"Are not five sparrows sold for two pennies? Yet not one of them is forgotten by God. Indeed, the very hairs of your head are all numbered. Don't be afraid; you are worth more than many sparrows" (Luke 12:6–7).

Grief and loss imploded the life I knew; grace and love rebuilt it. I say *rebuilt* because that is precisely what happened. And the catalyst wasn't tragedy, death, or the loss of my love—that was a destructive blow. Grace and love, both sowed by God into the shocked soil of my heart, sealed the seeping holes. God knew me. I felt it for the first time in a way much different and completely necessary. The pain, loneliness, betrayal, anger, confusion, and helplessness—He knew all about them. He is specifically familiar with the very hairs of my head, and He, too, knows the condition of my heart.

For weeks and months I smiled in response to the never-ending question of how I was doing. Most times, I didn't mean what I said. I knew that those asking didn't believe me. How could I be "okay"? How could my answer be convincing after such a grand undoing of the core of my life? But I smiled more for myself than for those asking. I needed to feel normal, like them, even though I was far from it. I was sinking in words scribbled on pages and bled into journals. The need to be okay called constantly from the confusion ringing in my heart. Each morning I woke to the worst dream while trying to ignore the ugliest parts. Call it a defense mechanism, denial, forced optimism, depression, or all of the above. A ship capsized and the captain was drowning, hands clasped tight to the wheel, hat pulled down tight, ankles, knees, and finally waist wet in the rising water of grief and the loneliness of loss.

I'll never forget one morning while I was driving. Everything seemed to grow louder . . . the sound of the road, the morning traffic around me, the oddest thoughts and the familiar ones.

I felt far from life.

I felt eerily close to death.

I felt betrayed and abandoned.

Tears began to stream down my face. The heaviness wasn't just burdensome and bulky, it was getting louder, demanding my attention. Finally, I had to pull over and do something. *Surely, I'll pray and the overwhelming feelings will subside,* I thought. I sat still under the weight and volume. I didn't know what to say or how to say it. All I did was cry. I had never felt so deeply hurt and lonely. Unable to pray, I fumbled for my journal to try to write. I just needed to let go of the pent-up pain. One word sat on the top of the blank page.

It was a curse, an epithet, a cry of raw rage.

The ugliness of the word glared at me. That one word rebelled against my life's values like fingernails digging into a chalkboard. But I couldn't wear a mask anymore and pretend everything was okay. The promises I had held so tightly didn't work. There was no healing, no restoration, and certainly no joy. Marianne was dead. It was the most painful fact of my life. Up to that point, I barely made it through each day. I was completely screwed up inside. For me, the entirety of hurt attached to that one word. All the horror and unbearable weight bound up in a written word that had always been off limits to me as a pastor. But it didn't matter. I had to be honest. It all converged at that moment in this ugly confession: the sadness, the anger, the fear, the hurt. I couldn't go one more step allowing God to exist only on the periphery of my darkest time.

The dramatic expletive didn't liberate or empower me. God did. God drew closer at my weakest. Grace found me there. He put my hand back into His. I knew that forever, I would be different. Forever, I will trust Him more. Forever, I will be braver. For God is exactly who I need Him to be, everything, and beyond all that I can imagine.

I learned that God is, indeed, fully capable and deeply loving during the most frightful stretches of our lives. He hunts for those who are broken and pursues those who have fallen. When all has failed, He meets us at our deepest places and heals our deepest wounds.

Grace is blocked when we play games and put on masks. It thrives when we find the courage to be honest with God.

I am dreaming of a new day,
swallowing tomorrow.
The bitterest taste lingers
only until the sweetness of something new.
Years fall gently like leaves carried by the wind
to a place whispered safely,
to a time called forever.
You are the reader, the author, the pen
turning pages with hands delicate,
write the words that will carry me to the end.

CHAPTER ELEVEN

Into Tomorrow, a Prologue

The cosmos and all that we do not know and cannot see,

the grandness of life still being discovered all around us,

living and breathing,

breath, and the rhythm of day,

heart, and its regular beat,

the mouth of an innocent child

smiling with unjust cause,

evidences littered on a path of shuffling feet,

whispers echoing, escaping from clouds descending,

grace invading the grotesque heaviness of life

and all that you know,

all that you thought you knew

kindly wiped away, a gentle destruction.

I REMEMBER THE moment clearly: the ending.

The doctor, a neurologist whom until this point I had never met, led me to a group of chairs in a sort of carved-out corner just down the hall from the ICU room. She pulled a curtain around us, creating a temporary room. I sat. My eyes tried to connect to hers. I waited for words to come. She sat unassumingly, shuffling through a small stack of papers as I held the question that had been hanging for days.

"What about my wife? Is she dead?"

I finally said it aloud to the person who could give me an answer.

In asking it, I felt a hollowness ringing as my words hung in the space between me and the doctor.

All I could think of was Marianne and the years behind us. They didn't seem like separate years numbering well more than a decade, but one seamless smile with the warmth of a lifetime. What we had together felt magical, even in the mundane. We had so much to be thankful for. I had been blessed, well beyond what I deserved.

In moments like these, life can be most peculiar. I glimpsed holy gratitude while sitting with a stranger, my toes curled on the edge of life, the divide of earth and sky, stretching as far as faith or hope or wishing could reach.

Unfortunately, thankfulness doesn't change medical realities.

We had only been apart one time before.

She left. It was an argument that neither of us even remembered later. She stormed out of our still unpacked apartment . . . in my jeep. At least she could have taken her car!

Still easing into our life together, the honeymoon only days behind us, we were stubbornly and defiantly insisting on our own ways of living. For whatever reason, we dug our heels in on this issue and neither of us planned to move an inch.

We were afraid of losing ourselves. It was silly and foolish. We were unaware of all that would be gained in the years ahead of us. I stood on the curb outside our apartment and watched her drive away. I realized that this new life together wouldn't be easy. Minutes crawled by. I sat on the curb under the night sky unable to call her, hoping she would come back.

I couldn't even remember the argument.

"I'm sorry," I softly whispered to her when she walked up. It was like a prayer.

"Me too."

Her voice startled me. Apparently, she had driven around the apartment complex but didn't actually leave. She parked the jeep and decided to walk around a bit. She ended up back at our building. The whole drama lasted no longer than thirty minutes, but it pulled together all that we were and would be.

We made a decision that night that would define "forever" for us. We committed to always be on the same side of the line, no matter what. If we were wrong, we would be wrong together. It would be Marianne and I through everything, thin and thick, always together. From that night, our vows, barely two weeks old, settled more deeply within us.

And I realized that life was just beginning.

Back in the hospital with the silent doctor, I shifted uncomfortably in an upright chair. The doctor's eyes lifted from the stack of papers in her hands.

After a long indefinite pause, almost carelessly and quite matter-of-factly, she spoke words that shoved through my heart.

"Mr. Delcambre, there are no signs . . . no evidence that your wife's brain is functioning. She is completely brain dead."

Silently, my heart shook and buried itself beneath the weight of her words. She continued.

"There's nothing that can be done. No treatment option. Without the brain, the body will certainly shut down and die. I'm sorry. Can I get someone for you?"

I didn't say a word. My heart broke.

The end.

She was gone.

This time she wouldn't be walking back to me. For the first time since that night outside our apartment filled with unpacked boxes, I stood on this side of the line alone and without her.

"No. No, thank you. Thank you for telling me."

And with that I pushed through the curtain half alive. I don't recall what happened next. Memories hung in the air. The day floated by in my consciousness. I wanted to fade beyond the reach of hugs and drown in tears.

· · · · ·

"Where I am most inwardly myself,
there You are far more than I."

—Augustine

Emmanuel. God with us.

In every moment, every impasse and turn, every bend and crook in the path, in the storm and the darkness, in the pulling and pushing and crushing of life, God is present. No matter the circumstance, tragedy, or difficulty, He stands ready and waiting to find, lift, and rescue.

Sun-warmed sky dawns as the horizon overcomes darkness. Birds chirp content with each new day. Creation stretches toward the sun and sky. Night turns to day, and the day celebrates life again. In each undoing, life derailing, and ending, there's a beginning. "I will never leave you nor forsake you." Not every beginning is chosen, welcomed, or understood. Some just happen in life's endings. Like a chapter you never want to finish, a story forever unfolding good, a warming visit with a friend or loved one. You hope there's no ending. But at some point all things end, succumbing to time or circumstance or consequence.

• • • • •

I stumbled into each day tightly holding the loss of my wife. For a while, it felt natural. I had to process her death in both my mind and my heart.

When do you stop grieving the loss of love? When is it over? When does life return to normal (whatever that is)? These questions plastered the walls of my heart and begged for answers . . . but I had none. With no satisfying answers, my loss consumed all of my time and thoughts. It shaped the new reality of life.

I didn't choose this new identity: victim.

Something took my life, the one that I knew well and loved, and gave back only half.

It wasn't fair.

It wasn't right.

I couldn't stand it.

But it defined me.

Every day, a solemn sound echoed in my heart. The sounds creaked in my chest and my head, but the wheels kept spinning. After Marianne died, each day ran over into the next one, leaving no end or beginning other than the sun filling the sky and the moon and stars glimmering in the dark.

But one thing stood out: the numbers. I could feel thirty days pass. And then sixty. And ninety. Six months, nine months . . . then twelve.

After a year, I could see that my life contained a few small pockets of happiness, but those brief, lighter moments soon gave way to the particular rhythm of days—wake up, cope, go to bed, repeat. Another day survived. Not every day was so heavy. Most days were numb.

For several weeks, I felt only the distance, not the forever. I remember the first time I woke with something to tell her. Half-awake, I found myself downstairs looking for her, only to find an empty coffee pot, a quiet house, and memories reverberating in every room. I looked at the spot at the counter where I would sit for a few moments while the coffee dripped. Every morning we talked about the most randomly intimate things that only we knew about each other. How I missed that.

Almost every morning, she warmed water in her electric kettle to dilute the morning coffee because I always made it too strong for her liking. She always tasted it before adding more water. She was always astonished that I had made it absurdly strong—far too strong for her.

And I looked at the chair she sank into with her Bible, journal, and weakened coffee.

The house was disturbingly quiet, but somehow it was still warm with those delicious memories. She had been there only a short time before. Before everything changed.

For a while, I had to remind myself that she was, in fact, gone and never returning. Not merely gone, like on a trip to Wisconsin or Egypt or Waco, but dead, existing now only in memories and stories. It was as if my mind couldn't fathom the concept of forever—or maybe I actively rejected it in disbelief.

She died, I reminded myself.

And even though I didn't say it aloud, I knew just as surely that a large part of me had died.

I'd been thirty-three, more than a decade into marriage, and sinking deeper into love and friendship. Joy had filled our lives, a deep satisfaction and hope for a wonderful future together. Suddenly I was changed against my will. I went to sleep a man held in place by a life he understood. I awoke a grieving widower hollowed by loss, and an overwhelmed single dad shuffling to make it through the day.

How did I get here? Some questions don't have answers of any kind. In the absence of any real answers, I held to hurt and quietly accused God of "allowing" this to happen as part of some greater good—His grand scheme. It seemed that I had to accept this new life as "just how things would be now."

I found no cause for joy or celebration. In fact, any form of true happiness felt completely wrong, a betrayal, a violation.

Why would I ever be happy? My fists closed around what I could control. I could permit myself to be happy in anything and everything regarding my daughters. After all, they had lost as much as I in her death—maybe more. I had shared a lifetime of love and joy in a compressed amount of time. They would never have that.

Their loss included grieving for me. It was unjust, and yet it was true and real and awful.

I determined to give them all I could and lead them to a place I wasn't sure I could inhabit: experiencing joy in life. My resolve to lead them away from brokenness to joy would have positive and unexpected consequences: it would lead me to joy, too. In hindsight, I wasn't doing much leading. They were.

Healing begins with hands opened.

Letting go allowed me to open my hands to grace, love, and healing. I found a new day of blossoming hope, whispers of life floating in and out like spring winds, and gentle showers reviving the crust of a heart left dry by winter winds.

In the deepest grief, the world is only and always about our pain. Our eyes see through dark filters. Questions cloud our hearts, and we recoil in distrust. Pain is real and tragedy hobbles us. When we hurt, the initial tendency is to pull back, to hang on to what we've lost with a death grip. If we stay there too long—if we refuse to open our hands, simultaneously letting go and grabbing on—we suffer a certain death in our souls.

Many people—including many Christians—don't understand grief at all. They think we should be "conquerors" and instantly "rise above" the pain. Or they have some romanticized notion that pain makes us nobler and stronger than ever, like wounded warriors.

Yes, we can be stronger than ever, but not soon, and not easily. The promises of simple, quick, smooth relief are lies—smoke and mirrors. Those misplaced expectations actually make the pain worse because they don't allow for genuine honesty and healing.

· · · · ·

"Faith is the one's persistent engagement in the efficacious reality of God . . . that dissolves the sense of 'I alone' for 'we together.'"

—James Houston

Inwardly I began to live again. God became more real than ever. He wasn't just a form in the sky, watching, guiding, and sometimes interacting. When I was more real with Him, I encountered Him as more real than I had ever dreamed.

It didn't happen quickly, and it wasn't easy. For a long time, I believed He owed me. I had measured God with scales of happiness, success, calm resolve, smooth waters, and a perfect, unaffected life. But that view of God didn't cut it when Marianne died. I needed more than a Santa Claus or a grandfather. I needed the sovereign King and Savior . . . nothing less and nothing else.

So many devoted people had prayed for my wife's healing. When God didn't come through with the answer we wanted, my concept of Him began to crumble. I blamed Him. Oh, I knew well enough that He wasn't the cause of Marianne's death, but He also didn't cause a miracle of healing. There was nothing. Only a quiet sky with emptiness, death, and heartache.

Faith took on a new form and substance in my life. I developed a learned optimism based on the presence of God. His heavenly promises became real, filtered through earthly effort and affection—mine. But it wasn't neat and clean. Grief isn't like that. I still struggled with the hurt, heartache, and stress circling around me. I realized I wasn't the center of the universe. My concepts of God, of life, and of myself all died as something far better began to grow.

I am a mere speck, a glowing flicker, a passing moment.

A lot was changing. Until that point, God had been a benign, distantly ambiguous form. I didn't need Him very much, and I didn't love Him very much. My life didn't demand faith, trust, or belief in anything outside of what I could control. Each day unfolded, compartmentalized and organized into a list that was defined by goals, expectations, desires, dreams, and fears. The promise of heaven became a packaged, rationalized part of my consciousness. At the center of it all, I shaped my world with moral cues and created rigid expectations.

Do this and expect that. Don't do that and get this.

It was a simplistic world, barely influenced by Jesus. My faith was a tool to get more of what I wanted. When I obeyed, I was sure I was earning points with God—and I intended to cash them in from time to time. I look back now and wonder at how shallow and selfish I had been.

I am.

Had to become . . .

I am not.

In the depths of my sorrow, God pursued me, found me, and introduced Himself to me. God is all and the source of every living thing, even (maybe especially) in life's darkest times. I found the real meaning of Paul's statement, "For when I am weak, then I am strong" (2 Corinthians 12:10). First, though, I had to admit I was weak. I had to admit that I wasn't in control of the universe, and God might have purposes far beyond anything I could imagine. I had to let go of my silly, selfish view of life and God. Only then could I experience His presence, His healing, and His joy.

His love is far bigger, wider, and deeper than anyone can imagine. I'll never grasp the full depth of God's tender and powerful love for me or the width of His limitless grace. I need His love and grace all day, every day. One experience isn't enough. I still find myself broken and hollow, foolish and selfish, full of self-pity and pride and blame . . . a real mess. But even there, God reaches to touch me and assure me again.

God became more real than anything else in my life. He moved from the periphery to the center. He holds my life in His hands—His strong, tender hands. He is deeply moved by our pain, but His love is unmovable and unchanging.

Tragedy awakened me. Love found me. Grace lifted me. God led me to shift Him out of my life as my waiter, my butler, or my co-pilot—and let Him reenter as the center and source of real life.

Heaven is my home. It's not just a place "out there somewhere." I live in the presence of God all day, every day—a reality that is far greater than comprehension and reasoning. The reality of God is more real and powerful than shifting circumstances, no matter how great the threat.

The distance between earth and sky, between me and God, diminished through the greatest wound I've ever endured. God reached and grace collided into the ugliest mess of a grieving heart. His grace invaded the grotesque heaviness of my life and radically altered all that I knew. It was a necessary destruction, but a gentle one.

To a great extent, grief is an act of faith. To move through a day, no matter the pace—shuffling, stumbling, falling, failing, tentatively, doubtful, or suspicious—is to hope.

At some primal level, those days speak softly of the potential to grow and thrive again. Hope is the seed of faith, and from it trust grows into strong branches. Grief is a natural, normal, inevitable response to loss. It's the only path to restore a broken heart.

Faith is our response to God. We may blame, scream, and cry, but faith keeps clinging to Him even when we receive no good answers. We may feel alone, but we trust He is there in our darkness.

In grieving, grace strengthened me every sinking moment, every day. Steadily, the pain dissolved. God descended into the mess, and loneliness gave way to belonging. Faith gradually grew, watered by continual grace. When yesterday crashes into today, beating relentlessly as waves carrying away pieces of the shore, sometimes all we can do is hang on for one more minute. That's all. And it's enough.

As time went by, I found new hope in shuffling one foot in front of the other. One step at a time birthed hope in a better future—somehow, somewhere, certainly. Each step creates a path through treacherous terrain. If we saw the whole path at once, we would be overwhelmed. But all we see is the next step. "Even though I walk through the valley of the shadow of death, I will fear no evil, for You are with me." That's faith, and that's grief, earth and sky colliding.

My brother died when he was only eight. I was five, and I didn't really get it. Even then, God was already at work to reframe my life with His truth and grace.

Even when I didn't see Him, God was there.

I found faith through fear in high school. God.

My hero dad left my mom in the slowest, clumsiest way. God.

I went off to college. I was lost and drifting. God.

I met the one who would become the one. God.

I defied my own odds and became a pastor. God.

The most wonderful person I've ever known had a heartfelt love for me. God.

We celebrated the births of our three great treasures. God.

I learned to be a father. God.

With a blend of fear and courage, we left comfort behind to pursue the thinnest of dreams together as a family. God.

Marianne died. God.

Life collapsed. God.

I held my daughters who were breaking in the dust of death. God.

Awakening to a new day. God.

Finding new life. God.

Writing. God.

Epilogue to prologue (backwards, I know). Ending to (re) beginning, in redemptive strokes. God.

Trusting, and not needing to have all the answers. God.

Many people believe in the *concept* of God. They think He exists out there somewhere, somehow holding everything together and keeping the world from tilting too far out of control. But He's not real and personal to them. They're comfortable with the distance because they're afraid being close will change too much in their lives. They've read the Bible stories! But when they're in need, a distant, impersonal God isn't enough. They need more. They need Him.

Some believe they have "tried God," but He didn't come through like they hoped He would. They wanted action, but all they got was silence. I know. I've been there. But He is here. He doesn't jump to our commands, and He doesn't meet all our expectations, but He is here in all of His wisdom, kindness, power, and mystery—all of that, and nothing less. If we let Him, God will meet us where we are. We will awaken to His presence and realize He has pursued us all along.

We feel like we have found Him, but He has found us. He always does.

How to Write a Grief Journal

MANY PEOPLE FIND IT helpful to write a journal to help them think more clearly as they grieve. I want to give some suggestions to steer you in a productive direction. First, let me share some perspectives about this awkward and awful (but necessary and healing) process of grieving.

When we experience loss, grief isn't optional. Earl Grollman observed, "Grief is not a disorder, a disease or a sign of weakness. It is an emotional, physical and spiritual necessity, the price you pay for love. The only cure for grief is to grieve." [2] And Doug Manning wrote, "You give yourself permission to grieve by recognizing the need for grieving. Grieving is the natural way of working through the loss of a love. Grieving is not weakness nor absence of faith. Grieving is as natural as crying when you are hurt, sleeping when you are tired or sneezing when your nose itches. It is nature's way of

---

2   Earl Grollman, *Straight Talk about Death for Teenagers* (Boston: Beacon Press, 1993), 6.

healing a broken heart." [3] If we try to avoid the pain of grief (and we all instinctively do), our hearts will stay broken. That's no way to live.

For decades, leaders in counseling have observed identifiable stages of grief. More recently, however, psychologists have recognized that these stages aren't quite as clear as they previously thought. It may be more helpful to describe contrasting approaches to loss: productive grief and blocked grief.

The beginning of both often looks similar. When we learn about the death of someone we love—whether it comes after a prolonged illness or was completely unexpected—we may feel stunned and confused. We may implode instantly in sadness and despair, or we may explode in rage and blame.

In this early encounter with loss, we often suffer from shock. We can't wrap our minds around what happened. We think, "This can't be true!" We're emotionally numb and mentally dense. For days, weeks, or even months, we may alternate between shock and despair, or shock and anger.

The urge to find someone to blame can overwhelm us. We blame the dead person for making bad choices that contributed to the death, we blame the doctors and nurses, and we may accuse family members of not doing enough. But many of us, especially those who are particularly sensitive, blame ourselves. We lash ourselves with vicious attacks, "If I'd only done this or that, it wouldn't have happened!" Blame seems so right, but it only creates deeper and longer lasting wounds.

---

3   Doug Manning, *Don't Take My Grief Away from Me* (Oklahoma City: In Sight Books, 2011), 66.

In this time, we often suffer from disturbances in our normal rhythms. We sleep too much or we can't sleep at all. We eat too much or we're never hungry. We bury ourselves in work and projects to stay busy or we sit and watch television for countless hours. We're irritable, depressed, and hopeless.

All of these aspects of grief are completely predictable. We're human, not machines, and our world has been shattered.

In productive grief, we admit all that's going on in our hearts and our lives. We find the courage to be honest with ourselves, with God, and with at least one other person. We don't feel guilty for crying, and we aren't ashamed to be lost in heartache. In all of our pain, we may want to push people away and wallow in self-pity and loneliness, but we make the phone call, meet with a friend, and connect with someone who understands.

Sooner or later, we learn to treasure wonderful memories. Telling stories about the one we've lost enables us to put shape to our loss. The stories remind us of the good times, but they reveal that we'll never enjoy those times again. Telling stories is a double-edged sword.

The stories lead us to find meaning—in the person who's gone, in the relationship, and in God's goodness in the midst of our pain. For a long time, we've asked, "Why?" But now we begin to ask, "What now?" We become more comfortable with ambiguity, with not having answers to our questions because we trust that God knows, God cares, and God can teach us life's most important lessons from the depths of our pain.

The process of productive grief isn't smooth or easy or quick. Some authorities say it takes two years to grieve a major loss. That doesn't mean we feel completely hopeless until that last day. We continue to grow, heal, and learn during that time. At last, the sting isn't as sharp. We've accepted the new, painful reality, and in fact, we realize we've grown stronger, wiser, and more compassionate. Accidental deaths take longer, and violent, criminal acts take longer, still. There is no formula, just a process—a long and crucial grieving process.

Many people, though, refuse to step onto the path of productive grief. They continue to live in self-pity or rage or some combination of intense feelings. They become emotionally paralyzed. They may be completely isolated, or they may crave attention. Their lives have been shattered—that's true—but they've lost hope. They've concluded there are no good stories, no meaning, and no people to walk with them through the darkness. They believe their sadness (or anger) will never end, and no one will ever understand them. They have to blame somebody, so they focus their venom on others or themselves. They're lost in their pain, and they can't see any way out.

For these people, their loss defines them and consumes their thoughts. C. S. Lewis wrote *A Grief Observed* to recount his responses to his wife's death. He realized that he not only thought about the loss, he also thought about thinking about the loss. He wrote, "I once read the sentence, 'I lay awake all night with a toothache, thinking about the toothache and about lying awake.' That's true to life. Part of every misery is, so to speak, the misery's shadow or reflection: the fact that you don't merely suffer but have to keep on thinking about the fact that you suffer. I not only live each endless day in grief, but live each day thinking about living each day in grief." [4]

That's a good description of at least one of the symptoms of blocked grief. The process of moving forward in productive grief, to be sure, often includes times—sometimes long periods—when it appears we're making no progress at all. We need people around us who have been down this road before and who will lovingly, patiently, and persistently take our hands and help us take the next step. I believe no one successfully makes the journey alone. We must have someone, but the right someone. We don't need anyone to smother us, feel for us, and think for us. But we need a trusted friend, pastor, or counselor to be the arms of grace and the voice of truth.

Unfortunately, many Christians feel uncomfortable with pain, loss, suffering, and grief. Their theology—or more probably, their comfort level—doesn't allow for prolonged seasons of healing, learning, and growing. They prefer instant answers, and they're sure God doesn't intend for anyone to hurt more than a day or so. This perspective would be a shock to the writers of the Psalms. More than half of those poems and songs of faith are "wintry." They depict honest displays of painful emotions, including deep disappointment with God, anger, despair, fear, and the rest of human feelings. In all but a couple of the Psalms, the writer finally comes to the conclusion that God is faithful, kind, and strong, but we have no idea how long the process took to come to that point. Actually, it doesn't matter how long it takes. God is much more interested in developing genuine faith than rushing our schedules.

---

4   C. S. Lewis, *A Grief Observed* (London: Faber and Faber, 1961), 10–11.

Superficial, simplistic, spiritual answers won't cut it. They may sound good at first, but they leave the grieving person feeling even more disappointed when the quick relief doesn't last (or doesn't happen at all).

The body of Christ can be a healing community. A few years ago, Philip Yancey was asked to speak at a memorial service after a gunman murdered students at Virginia Tech. He told them,

> "I wish I could say that the pain you feel will disappear, vanish, never to return. I'm sure you've heard comments like these from parents and others: 'Things will get better.' 'You'll get past this.' 'This too shall pass.' Those who offer such comfort mean well, and it's true that what you feel now you will not always feel. Yet it's also true that [the impact of the murders] will stay with you forever. You are a different person because of that day, because of one troubled young man's actions. In grief, love and pain converge. [The gunman] felt no grief as he gunned down your classmates because he had no love for them. You feel grief because you did have a connection. Some of you had closer ties to the victims, but all of you belong to a body to which they too belonged. When that body suffers, you suffer. Remember that as you cope with the pain. Don't try to numb it. Instead, acknowledge it as a perception of life and of love." [5]

---

5   "Where Is God When It Hurts?," Philip Yancey, *Christianity Today,* June 6, 2007, www.christianitytoday.com/ct/2007/june/14.55.html

Through it all, we need to connect with God—some of us for the first time, most of us in a deeper way than ever before. It seems like He's a million miles away, or worse, that He's close but indifferent. He's neither distant nor indifferent. The most common emotion mentioned in the life of Jesus is "compassion." It means that He felt others' pain as His own. He still does. He weeps with us when we cry, He's angry at the injustice we've endured, and He tenderly reaches out to touch us at the point of our deepest pain. He's here. We can count on it. C. S. Lewis assures us, "God whispers to us in our pleasures, speaks in our conscience, but shouts in our pains: it is His megaphone to rouse a deaf world." [6]

I'm giving you a few questions and prompts to stir your heart, focus your mind, and direct your steps down the road of productive grief. Let me warn you: journaling can be wonderfully therapeutic, but can be terribly threatening. Take your time, but be diligent. It's not a race, and your goal isn't to check off boxes. I recommend that you get a notebook and begin writing your thoughts and answers to these questions. You'll resist some of them. That's fine. You can come back to those later when you feel stronger. You don't have to write in complete sentences. (I didn't!) Just pour your heart out on paper. Answer one or two at a time.

Before you begin each time, ask God to give you a sense of His presence and kindness. Remember the compassion of Jesus and make it your own.

After you've completed the cycle of these questions, come back and do it again . . . maybe several times. You'll go through layers of grief and healing. It's part of the process. Whatever you do, don't

---

6   C. S. Lewis, *The Problem of Pain* (New York: Macmillan, 1962), 93.

give up on God. Take breaks, ride a bike, hang out with friends, and forget the pain for a while, but come back to the process. Don't let the pain fester deep in your soul and poison you.

Be kind to yourself at every moment. You've been through a lot, and you need a break. But you also need the courage to take the next step no matter where it leads.

Deep breath in . . . and now exhale and begin to open your eyes to a new day where all behind you is held by grace and all ahead warmed by hope.

1. What happened? Describe the person you lost and the details of the loss. Were you surprised?
2. How did you respond initially?
3. How would you describe the shock of the loss?
4. Did you emotionally implode or explode? Describe it.
5. Did you experience disruption of sleep, eating, work, or relationships? Explain what happened and how you're doing now.
6. Did you withdraw from people or cling to them? How about now?
7. Did you look for someone—anyone—to blame? How did that work for you? How is it working for you?
8. What does blocked grief look like? How does hopelessness feel?
9. What feelings are you experiencing now? How intense are they?

10. Who has been there for you? How have they helped you through the darkest moments? Write a thank you note to the person (or several of them).
11. What do you wish they had done for you?
12. What gives you a sense of pleasure and hope at this point?
13. What memories of the person do you cherish?
14. How do you feel when you tell those stories? (Have you told them or only thought them?)
15. What are some passages of Scripture that have been particularly meaningful to you as you've been grieving? Which ones seem empty and wrong?
16. Why is asking "Why?" natural but not productive? How is "What now?" a much better question?
17. Have you found slivers of meaning in your grieving process? What are some lessons you've learned or are learning?
18. For weeks or months, you can complete these statements every day:
—Today, I'm feeling . . .
—I want . . .
—I can't control . . .
—I can control . . .
—God seems . . .
—I trust Him to . . .
—The next step for me is . . .

Acknowledgements

THE WRITER WITHIN ME would still be a shadowed dream were it not for Ben Arment and his inspirational genius. I'm not sure this book would have been written without our conversations. Thank you for helping me believe this story should absolutely be told. Without your help, I would undoubtedly still be scribbling emotions into a journal in a cabin somewhere.

I'm deeply thankful to the entire team at Influence Resources and to Steve and Susan Blount who were encouraging and believing. And to Sarah Cunningham for patiently working through my manuscript to straighten bending thoughts, thank you. I'm grateful to Pat Springle for your keen insights that added appropriate balance to my story.

I'm thankful to you, Mom, for your constant support and undying belief in God's work in all circumstance.

Thank you to those shoulders who lowered to lift me at my weakest: Steve Flores for driving more than the miles you did. Your friendship is gold. Mel and Kim Masengale, Justin and Casey Graves, Shannon and Cassandra Dalrymple, Gary and Andrea Humble—your friendship transcends what once was. A depth of gratitude to Erik Hebert for finding a place for me and my daughters to heal. Thank you to Duane Litwick and Erik Lind for the adventures that will always live on; and to John Finch for dreaming out of the neighborhood with me; and to Shawn Reine, a giant of a friend with the roar of a grizzly. Your simple relentlessness never ceases to inspire me.

Thank you to Justin Lathrop, Art House Dallas, the Deeper Story family, Larry Barber, Rob Pine, and each of the wonderful volunteers at Grief Works. Thank you to Brian Brooks of Innovado. net and Evan Mann (evanmann.com) for your amazing illustration and collaborative work.

A forever thank you to New Life Church in my hometown of Abbeville, Louisiana, and Journey Church in Denton, Texas, for giving me the space to wrestle with and be owned by God's hunting love and immeasurable grace. Thank you to Matt Chandler and the Village Church for giving us a home to settle into and grow with.

And finally, a continually deepening gratitude to Marissa for your fierce love of our bruised hearts. Each time I read love in your eyes, I thank God for His fullness.

About the Author

GUY MARTIN DELCAMBRE is an author and public speaker based in Dallas, Texas, who writes about faith in thin moments, strength found in weakness, and God's grace immeasurable. Guy was once a pastor, a church planter, and a widower, in that order. From the darkest night in life, the death of a spouse, to learning to live life as a single father to three young daughters, Guy traveled the greatest distance of the heart to find home in God's faithful goodness.

He lives with his wife, Marissa, and three daughters, Elizabeth, Emily, and Chloe.

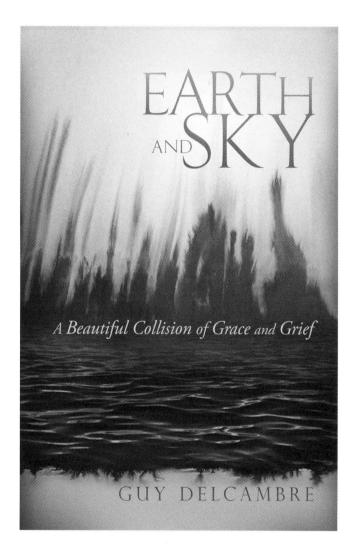

EARTH
AND SKY

A Beautiful Collision of Grace and Grief

GUY DELCAMBRE

For more information about this book,

visit www.influenceresources.com